Carl Engel

Musical Instruments

Carl Engel

Musical Instruments

ISBN/EAN: 9783743345973

Manufactured in Europe, USA, Canada, Australia, Japa

Cover: Foto ©Thomas Meinert / pixelio.de

Manufactured and distributed by brebook publishing software (www.brebook.com)

Carl Engel

Musical Instruments

SOUTH KENSINGTON MUSEUM ART HANDBOOKS.

EDITED BY WILLIAM MASKELL.

No. 5.—MUSICAL INSTRUMENTS.

These Handbooks are reprints of the dissertations prefixed to the large catalogues of the chief divisions of works of art in the Museum at South Kensington; arranged and so far abridged as to bring each into a portable shape. The Lords of the Committee of Council on Education having determined on the publication of them, the editor trusts that they will meet the purpose intended; namely, to be useful, not alone for the collections at South Kensington but for other collections, by enabling the public at a trifling cost to understand something of the history and character of the subjects treated of.

The authorities referred to in each book are given in the large catalogues; where will also be found detailed descriptions of the very numerous examples in the South Kensington Museum.

W. M.

August, 1875.

SICAL INSTRUMENTS

BY

CARL ENGEL

WITH NUMEROUS WOODCUTS

Published for the Committee of Council on Education

BY

HAPMAN AND HALL, Ltd., LONDON.

LIST OF WOODCUTS.

	PAGE
Prehistoric whistle	9
Ancient Egyptian flute concert	13
The supposed Hebrew lyre at Beni Hassan	22
Ancient bagpipe from Tarsus	24
Hebrew trumpets, from the arch of Titus	25
Grecian harp and lyre	28
Greek lyres	29
Greek flutes	31
The *diaulos*	32
Etruscan *cornu*	33
Hydraulic organ	34
Roman girl and *tibia*	36
Roman trumpets	36
Chinese king	39
,, pien-tchung	41
,, hiuen-tchung	42
,, ou	43
,, tchou	43
,, kin-kou	44
,, hiuen	45
,, cheng	46

	PAGE
Hindustan, vina	49
Persian, chang	51
,, bagpipe	52
Turkish harp	53
Persian dulcimer	55
The *rebab*	56
Aztec whistles	60
Antique pipe from central America	61
Pipes of the Aztecs	62
Peruvian bone pipe	64
,, huayra-puhura	65
,, ,,	66
Orinoco Indian trumpet	67
South American Juruparis	68
Indian trumpets	70
Aztec drums	72
San Domingo drum	73
Peruvian bell	75
Aztec cluster of bells	76
Cithara, ninth century	86
Psalterium	87
Nablum	87
Citole	88
Anglo-saxon harp	89
Harp, ninth century	90
Ancient Irish harp	91
German rotte	91
Rotta	92
Irish rotta	93
The crwth	94
The old English "crowd"	95

	PAGE
The French crout	96
Anglo-saxon fiddle	97
German fiddle, ninth century	97
Organistrum	99
Monochord	100
Single chorus	101
Double chorus	101
Sackbut	101
Syrinx	102
Pneumatic organ, fourth century	103
Organ, twelfth century	104
Regal	104
Cymbalum, ninth century	105
Bunibulum	106
Orchestra on bas-relief	108
Vielle	109
Orchestra, twelfth century, at Santiago	110
The minstrels' gallery, at Exeter cathedral	112
Virginal	114
Lute, Elizabethan	116
Viola da gamba	118
Recorder	119
Scotch bagpipe, eighteenth century	120
Irish bagpipe, sixteenth century	121
Carillon, Netherlands	122

MUSICAL INSTRUMENTS.

CHAPTER I.

Music, in however primitive a stage of development it may be with some nations, is universally appreciated as one of the Fine Arts. The origin of vocal music may have been coeval with that of language; and the construction of musical instruments evidently dates with the earliest inventions which suggested themselves to human ingenuity. There exist even at the present day some savage tribes in Australia and South America who, although they have no more than the five first numerals in their language and are thereby unable to count the fingers of both hands together, nevertheless possess musical instruments of their own contrivance, with which they accompany their songs and dances.

Wood, metal, and the hide of animals, are the most common substances used in the construction of musical instruments. In tropical countries bamboo or some similar kind of cane and gourds are especially made use of for this purpose. The ingenuity of man has contrived to employ in producing music, horn, bone, glass, pottery, slabs of sonorous stone,—in fact, almost all vibrating matter. The strings of instruments have been made of the hair of animals, of silk, the runners of creeping plants, the fibrous roots of certain trees, of cane, catgut (which absurdly referred to the cat, is from the sheep, goat, lamb, camel, and some other animals), metal, &c.

The mode in which individual nations or tribes are in the habit of embellishing their musical instruments is sometimes as characteristic as it is singular. The negroes in several districts of western Africa affix to their drums human skulls. A war-trumpet of the king of Ashantee which was brought to England is surrounded by human jawbones. The Maories in New Zealand carve around the mouth-hole of their trumpets a figure intended, it is said, to represent female lips. The materials for ornamentation chiefly employed by savages are bright colours, beads, shells, grasses, the bark of trees, feathers, stones, gilding, pieces of looking-glass inlaid like mosaic, &c. Uncivilized nations are sure to consider anything which is bright and glittering ornamental, especially if it is also scarce. Captain Tuckey saw in Congo a negro instrument which was ornamented with part of the broken frame of a looking-glass, to which were affixed in a semicircle a number of brass buttons with the head of Louis XVI. on them,—perhaps a relic of some French sailor drowned near the coast years ago.

Again, musical instruments are not unfrequently formed in the shape of certain animals. Thus, a kind of harmonicon of the Chinese represents the figure of a crouching tiger. The Burmese possess a stringed instrument in the shape of an alligator. Even more grotesque are the imitations of various beasts adopted by the Javanese. The natives of New Guinea have a singularly shaped drum, terminating in the head of a reptile. A wooden rattle like a bird is a favourite instrument of the Indians of Nootka Sound. In short, not only the inner construction of the instruments and their peculiar quality of sound exhibit in most nations certain distinctive characteristics, but it is also in great measure true as to their outward appearance.

An arrangement of the various kinds of musical instruments in a regular order, beginning with that kind which is the most universally known and progressing gradually to the least usual, gives the following results. Instruments of percussion of indefinite sonorousness or, in other words, pulsatile instruments which have not a sound of a fixed pitch, as the drum, rattle, castanets, &c.,

are most universal. Wind instruments of the flute kind,—including pipes, whistles, flutes, Pandean pipes, &c.—are also to be found almost everywhere.

Much the same is the case with wind instruments of the trumpet kind. These are often made of the horns, bones, and tusks of animals; frequently of vegetable substances and of metal. Instruments of percussion of definite sonorousness are chiefly met with in China, Japan, Burmah, Siam, and Java. They not unfrequently contain a series of tones produced by slabs of wood or metal, which are beaten with a sort of hammer, as our harmonicon is played.

Stringed instruments without a finger board, or any similar contrivance which enables the performer to produce a number of different tones on one string, are generally found among nations whose musical accomplishments have emerged from the earliest state of infancy. The strings are twanged with the fingers or with a piece of wood, horn, metal, or any other suitable substance serving as a *plectrum;* or are made to vibrate by being beaten with a hammer, as our dulcimer. Stringed instruments provided with a finger-board on which different tones are producible on one string by the performer shortening it more or less,—as on the guitar and violin,—are met with almost exclusively among nations in a somewhat advanced stage of musical progress. Such as are played with a bow are the least common; they are, however, known to the Chinese, Japanese, Hindus, Persians, Arabs, and a few other nations, besides those of Europe and their descendants in other countries.

Wind instruments of the organ kind,—*i.e.*, such as are constructed of a number of tubes which can be sounded together by means of a common mouthpiece or some similar contrivance, and upon which therefore chords **and** combinations of chords, **or** harmony, can be produced,—are comparatively of rare occurrence. Some interesting specimens of them exist in China, Japan, Laos, and Siam.

Besides these various kinds of sound-producing means employed in musical performances, a few others less widely diffused could be pointed out, which are of a construction not represented in any of our well-known European specimens. For instance, some nations have peculiar instruments of friction, which can hardly be classed with our instruments of percussion. Again, there are contrivances in which a number of strings are caused to vibrate by a current of air, much as is the case with the Æolian harp; which might with equal propriety be considered either as stringed instruments or as wind instruments. In short, our usual classification of all the various species into three distinct divisions, viz. *Stringed Instruments, Wind Instruments,* and *Instruments of Percussion,* is not tenable if we extend our researches over the whole globe.

The collection at South Kensington contains several foreign instruments which cannot fail to prove interesting to the musician. Recent investigations have more and more elicited the fact that the music of every nation exhibits some distinctive characteristics which may afford valuable hints to a composer or performer. A familiarity with the popular songs of different countries is advisable on account of the remarkable originality of the airs: these mostly spring from the heart. Hence the natural and true expression, the delightful health and vigour by which they are generally distinguished. Our more artificial compositions are, on the other hand, not unfrequently deficient in these charms, because they often emanate from the fingers or the pen rather than from the heart. Howbeit, the predominance of expressive melody and effective rhythm over harmonious combinations, so usual in the popular compositions of various nations, would alone suffice to recommend them to the careful attention of our modern musicians. The same may be said with regard to the surprising variety in construction and in manner of expression prevailing in the popular songs and dance-tunes of different countries. Indeed, every nation's musical effusions exhibit a character peculiarly their own, with which the musician would find it advantageous to familiarize himself.

Now, it will easily be understood that an acquaintance with the musical instruments of a nation conveys a more correct idea than could otherwise be obtained of the characteristic features of the nation's musical compositions. Furthermore, in many instances the construction of the instruments reveals to us the nature of the musical intervals, scales, modulations, and suchlike noteworthy facts. True, inquiries like these have hitherto not received from musicians the attention which they deserve. The adepts in most other arts are in this respect in advance. They are convinced that useful information may be gathered by investigating the productions even of uncivilized nations, and by thus tracing the gradual progress of an art from its primitive infancy to its highest degree of development.

Again, from an examination of the musical instruments of foreign nations we may derive valuable hints for the improvement of our own; or even for the invention of new. Several principles of construction have thus been adopted by us from eastern nations. For instance, the *free reed* used in the harmonium is an importation from China. The organ builder Kratzenstein, who lived in St. Petersburg during the reign of Catharine II., happened to see the Chinese instrument *cheng*, which is of this construction, and it suggested to him, about the end of the last century, to apply the *free reed* to certain organ stops. At the present day instruments of the harmonium class have become such universal favourites in western Europe as almost to compete with the pianoforte.

Several other well-authenticated instances could be cited in which one instrument has suggested the construction of another of a superior kind. The prototype of our pianoforte was evidently the dulcimer, known at an early time to the Arabs and Persians who call it *santir*. One of the old names given to the dulcimer by European nations is *cimbal*. The Poles at the present day call it *cymbaly*, and the Magyars in Hungary *cimbalom*. The *clavicembalo*, the predecessor of the pianoforte, was in fact nothing but a *cembalo* with a key-board attached to it; and some of the old *clavicembali*, still preserved, exhibit the trapezium shape, the round hole in the middle of the sound-board, and other peculiarities of the first dulcimer. Again, the gradual development of the dulcimer from a rude contrivance, consisting merely of a wooden board across which a few strings are stretched, is distinctly traceable by a reference to the musical instruments of nations in different stages of civilization. The same is the case with our highly perfected harp, of which curious specimens, representing the instrument in its most primitive condition, are still to be found among several barbarous tribes. We might perhaps infer from its shape that it originally consisted of nothing more than an elastic stick bent by a string. The Damaras, a native tribe of South-western Africa, actually use their bow occasionally as a musical instrument, when they are not engaged in war or in the chase. They tighten the string nearly in the middle by means of a leathern thong, whereby they obtain two distinct sounds, which, for want of a sound-board, are of course very weak and scarcely audible to anyone but the performer. Some neighbouring tribes, however, possess a musical instrument very similar in appearance to the bow, to which they attach a gourd, hollowed and open at the top, which serves as a sound-board. Again, other African tribes have a similar instrument, superior in construction only inasmuch as it contains more than one string, and is provided with a sound-board consisting of a suitable piece of sonorous wood. In short, the more improved we find these contrivances the closer they approach our harp. And it could be shown if this were requisite for our present purpose that much the same gradual progress towards perfection, which we observe in the African harp, is traceable in the harps of several nations in different parts of the world.

Moreover, a collection of musical instruments deserves the attention of the ethnologist as much as of the musician. Indeed, this may be asserted of national music in general; for it gives us an insight into the heart of man, reveals to us the feelings and predilections of different races on the globe, and affords us a clue to the natural affinity which exists between different families of men. Again, a collection must prove interesting in a historical point of view. Scholars will find among old instruments specimens which were in common use in England at the time of queen Elizabeth, and which are not unfrequently mentioned in the literature of that period. In many instances the passages in which allusion is made to them can hardly be understood, if we are unacquainted with the shape and construction of the instruments. Furthermore, these relics of bygone times bring before our eyes the manners and customs of our forefathers, and assist us in understanding them correctly.

It will be seen that the modification which our orchestra has undergone, in the course of scarcely more than a century, is great indeed. Most of the instruments which were highly popular about a hundred years ago have either fallen into disuse or are now so much altered that they may almost be considered as new inventions. Among Asiatic nations, on the other hand, we meet with several instruments which have retained unchanged through many centuries their old construction and outward appearance. At South Kensington may be seen instruments still in use in Egypt and western Asia, precisely like specimens represented on monuments dating from a period of three thousand years ago. By a reference to the eastern instruments of the present time we obtain therefore a key for investigating the earlier Egyptian and Assyrian representations of musical performances; and, likewise, for appreciating more exactly the biblical records respecting the music of the Hebrews. Perhaps these evidences will convey to some inquirers a less high opinion than they have hitherto entertained, regarding the musical accomplishments of the Hebrew bands in the solemn processions of king David or in Solomon's temple; but the opinion will be all the nearer to the truth.

There is another point of interest about such collections, and especially that at **South** Kensington, which **must** not **be** left unnoticed. Several instruments are remarkable on account of their elegant shape and tasteful ornamentation. This is particularly the case with some specimens from Asiatic countries. **The beautiful designs** with which they are embellished may afford valuable patterns for study and for adoption in works of art.

CHAPTER II.

A REALLY complete account of all the musical instruments from the earliest time known to us would require much more space than can here be afforded. We can attempt only a concise historical survey. We venture to hope that the illustrations interspersed throughout the text will to the intelligent reader elucidate many facts which, for the reason stated, are touched upon but cursorily.

PRE-HISTORIC RELICS.

A musical relic has recently been exhumed in the department of Dordogne in France, which was constructed in an age when the fauna of France included the reindeer, the rhinoceros, and the mammoth, the hyæna, the bear, and the cave-lion. It is a small bone somewhat less than two inches in length, in which is a hole, evidently bored by means of one of the little flint knives which men used before acquaintance with the employment of metal for tools and weapons.

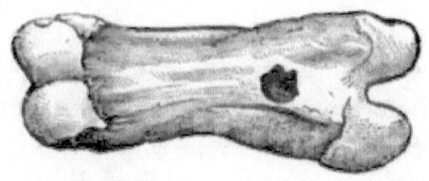

Many of these flints were found in the same place with the bones. Only about half a dozen of the bones, of which a considerable number have been exhumed, possess the artificial hole. We give a woodcut of one of them.

M. Lartet surmises the perforated bone to have been used as a whistle in hunting animals. It is the first digital phalanx of a ruminant, drilled to a certain depth by a smooth cylindrical bore on its lower surface near the expanded upper articulation. On applying it to the lower lip and blowing into it a shrill sound is yielded. Three of these phalanges are of reindeer, one is of chamois. Again, among the relics which have been brought to light from the cave of Lombrive, in the department of Ariège, occur several eye-teeth of the dog which have a hole drilled into them near the root. Probably they also yield sounds like those reindeer bones, or like the tube of a key. Another whistle—or rather a pipe, for it has three finger-holes by means of which different tones could be produced—was found in a burying-place, dating from the stone period, in the vicinity of Poitiers in France: it is rudely constructed from a fragment of stag's-horn. It is blown at the end, like a *flûte à bec*, and the three finger-holes are placed equidistantly. Four distinct tones must have been easily obtainable on it: the lowest, when all the finger-holes were covered; the other three, by opening the finger-holes successively. From the character of the stone utensils and weapons discovered with this pipe it is conjectured that the burying-place from which it was exhumed dates from the latest time of the stone age. Therefore, however old it may be, it is a more recent contrivance than the reindeer-bone whistle from the cavern of the Dordogne.

THE ANCIENT EGYPTIANS.

The most ancient nations historically known possessed musical instruments which, though in acoustic construction greatly inferior to our own, exhibit a degree of perfection which could have been attained only after a long period of cultivation. Many tribes of the present day have not yet reached this stage of musical progress.

As regards the instruments of the ancient Egyptians we now possess perhaps more detailed information than of those appertaining to any other nation of antiquity. This information we owe especially to the exactness with which the instruments are depicted in sculptures and paintings. Whoever has examined these interesting monuments with even ordinary care cannot but be convinced that the representations which they exhibit are faithful transcripts from life. Moreover, if there remained any doubt respecting the accuracy of the representations of the musical instruments it might be dispelled by existing evidence. Several specimens have been discovered in tombs preserved in a more or less perfect condition.

The Egyptians possessed various kinds of harps, some of which were elegantly shaped and tastefully ornamented. The largest were about six and a half feet high; and the small ones frequently had some sort of stand which enabled the performer to play upon the instrument while standing. The name of the harp was *buni*. Its frame had no front pillar; the tension of the strings therefore cannot have been anything like so strong as on our present harp.

The Egyptian harps most remarkable for elegance of form and elaborate decoration are the two which were first noticed by Bruce, who found them painted in fresco on the wall of a sepulchre at Thebes, supposed to be the tomb of Rameses III. who reigned about 1250 B.C. Bruce's discovery created sensation among the musicians. The fact that at so remote an age the Egyptians should have possessed harps which vie with our own in elegance and beauty of form appeared to some so incredible that the correctness of Bruce's representations, as engraved in his "Travels," was greatly doubted. Sketches of the same harps, taken subsequently and at different times from the frescoes, have since been published, but they differ more or less from each other in appearance and in the number of strings. A kind of triangular harp of the Egyptians was discovered in a well-preserved condition and is now deposited in the Louvre. It has twenty-one strings; a greater number than is generally represented on the monuments. All these instruments, however much they differed from each other in form, had one peculiarity in common, namely the absence of the fore pillar.

The *nofre*, a kind of guitar, was almost identical in construction with the Tamboura at the present day in use among several eastern nations. It was evidently a great favourite with the ancient Egyptians. A figure of it is found among their hieroglyphs, signifying "good." It occurs in representations of concerts dating earlier than from B.C. 1500. The *nofre* affords the best proof that the Egyptians had made considerable progress in music at a very early age; since it shows that they understood how to produce on a few strings, by means of the finger-board, a greater number of notes than were obtainable even on their harps. The instrument had two or four strings, was played with a plectrum and appears to have been sometimes, if not always, provided with frets. In the British museum is a fragment of a fresco obtained from a tomb at Thebes, on which two female performers on the *nofre* are represented. The painter has distinctly indicated the frets.

Small pipes of the Egyptians have been discovered, made of reed, with three, four, five, or more finger-holes. There are some interesting examples in the British museum; one of which has seven holes burnt in at the side. Two straws were found with it of nearly the same length as the pipe, which is about one foot long. In some other pipes pieces of a kind of thick straw have also been found inserted into the tube, obviously serving for a similar purpose as the *reed* in our oboe or clarionet.

The *sêbi*, a single flute, was of considerable length, and the performer appears to have been obliged to extend his arms almost at full length in order to reach the furthest finger-hole. As *sêbi* is also the name of the leg-bone (like the Latin *tibia*) it may be supposed that the Egyptian flute was originally made of bone. Those, however, which have been found are of wood or reed.

A flute-concert is painted on one of the tombs in the pyramids of Gizeh and dates, according to Lepsius, from an age earlier than B.C. 2000. Eight musicians (as seen in the woodcut) are performing on flutes. Three of them, one behind the other, are kneeling and holding their flutes in exactly the same manner. Facing these are three others, in a precisely similar position. A seventh is sitting on the ground to the left of the six, with his back turned towards them, but also in the act of blowing his flute, like the others. An eighth is standing at the right side of the group with his face turned towards them, holding his flute before him with both hands, as if he were going to put it to his mouth, or had just left off playing. He is clothed, while the others have only a narrow girdle round their loins. Perhaps he is the director of this singular band, or the *solo* performer who is waiting for the termination of the *tutti* before renewing his part of the performance. The division of the players into two sets, facing each other, suggests the possibility that the instruments were classed somewhat like the first and second violins, or the *flauto primo* and *flauto secondo* of our orchestras. The occasional employment of the interval of the third, or the fifth, as accompaniment to the melody, is not unusual even with nations less advanced in music than were the ancient Egyptians.

The Double-Pipe, called *mam*, appears to have been a very popular instrument, if we judge from the frequency of its occurrence in the representations of musical performances. Furthermore, the Egyptians had, as far as is known to us, two kinds of trumpets; three kinds of tambourines, or little hand drums; three kinds of drums, chiefly barrel-shaped; and various kinds of gongs, bells, cymbals, and castanets. The trumpet appears to have been usually of brass. A peculiar wind-instrument, somewhat the shape of a champagne bottle and perhaps made of pottery or wood, occurs only once in the representations transmitted to us.

The Egyptian drum was from two to three feet in length, covered with parchment at both ends and braced by cords. The performer carried it before him, generally by means of a band over his shoulder, while he was beating it with his hands on both ends. Of another kind of drum an actual specimen has been found in the excavations made in the year 1823 at Thebes. It was 1½ feet high and 2 feet broad, and had cords for bracing it. A piece of catgut encircled each end of the drum, being wound round each cord, by means of which the cords could be tightened or slackened at pleasure by pushing the two bands of catgut towards or from each other. It was beaten with two drumsticks slightly bent. The Egyptians had also straight drumsticks with a handle, and a knob at the end. The Berlin museum possesses some of these. The third kind of drum was almost identical with the *darabouka* (or *darabukkeh*) of the modern Egyptians. The Tambourine was either round, like that which is at the present time in use in Europe as well as in the east; or it was of an oblong square shape, slightly incurved on the four sides.

The Sistrum consisted of a frame of bronze or brass into which three or four metal bars were loosely inserted, so as to produce a jingling noise when the instrument was shaken. The bars were often made in the form of snakes, or they terminated in the head of a goose. Not unfrequently a few metal rings were strung on the bars, to increase the noise. The frame was sometimes ornamented with the figure of a cat. The largest sistra which have been found are about eighteen inches in length, and the smallest about nine inches. The sistrum was principally used by females in religious performances. Its Egyptian name was *seshesh*.

The Egyptian cymbals closely resembled our own in shape. There are two pairs of them in the British museum. One pair was found in a coffin enclosing the mummy of a sacred musician, and is deposited in the same case with the mummy and coffin. Among the Egyptian antiquities in the British museum are also several small bells of bronze. The largest is $2\frac{1}{4}$ inches in height, and the smallest three-quarters of an inch. Some of them have a hole at the side near the top wherein the clapper was fastened.

CHAPTER III.

THE ASSYRIANS.

OUR acquaintance with the Assyrian instruments has been derived almost entirely from the famous bas-reliefs which have been excavated from the mounds of Nimroud, Khorsabad, and Kouyunjik, situated near the river Tigris in the vicinity of the town of Mosul in Asiatic Turkey.

The Assyrian harp was about four feet high, and appears of larger size than it actually was on account of the ornamental appendages which were affixed to the lower part of its frame. It must have been but light in weight, since we find it not unfrequently represented in the hands of persons who are playing upon it while they are dancing. Like all the Oriental harps, modern as well as ancient, it was not provided with a front pillar. The upper portion of the frame contained the sound-holes, somewhat in the shape of an hour-glass. Below them were the screws, or tuning-pegs, arranged in regular order. The strings were perhaps made of silk, like those which the Burmese use at the present time on their harps; or they may have been of catgut, which was used by the ancient Egyptians.

The largest assemblage of Assyrian musicians which has been discovered on any monument consists of eleven performers upon instruments, besides a chorus of singers. The first musician—probably the leader of the band, as he marches alone at the head of the procession—is playing upon a harp. Behind him are two men; one with a dulcimer and the other with a double-pipe: then follow two men with harps. Next come six female musicians, four of whom are playing upon harps, while one is blowing a double-pipe and another is beating a small hand-drum covered only at the top. Close behind the instrumental performers are the singers, consisting of a chorus of females and children. They are clapping their hands in time with the music, and some of the musicians are dancing to the measure. One of the female singers is holding her hand to her throat in the same manner as the women in Syria, Arabia, and Persia are in the habit of doing at the present day when producing, on festive occasions, those peculiarly shrill sounds of rejoicing which have been repeatedly noticed by travellers.

The dulcimer is in too imperfect a state on the bas-relief to familiarize us with its construction. The slab representing the procession in which it occurs has been injured; the defect which extended over a portion of the dulcimer has been repaired, and it cannot be said that in repairing it much musical knowledge has been evinced.

The instrument of the Trigonon species was held horizontally, and was twanged with a rather long plectrum slightly bent at the end at which it was held by the performer. It is of frequent occurrence on the bas-reliefs. A number of them appear to have been generally played together. At any rate, we find almost invariably on the monuments two together, evidently implying " more than one," " a number." The left hand of the performer seems to have been occupied in checking the vibration of the strings when its discontinuance was required. From the position of the strings the performer could not have struck them as those of the dulcimer are struck. If he did not twang them, he may have drawn the plectrum across them. Indeed, for twanging, a short plectrum would have been more practical, considering that the strings are placed horizontally one above the other at regular distances. It is therefore by no means improbable that we have here a rude prototype of the violin bow.

The Lyre occurs in three different forms, and is held horizon-

C

tally in playing, or at least nearly so. Its front bar was generally either oblique or slightly curved. The strings were tied round the bar so as to allow of their being pushed upwards or downwards. In the former case the tension of the strings increases, and the notes become therefore higher; on the other hand, if the strings are pushed **lower** down the pitch of the notes must become deeper. The lyre was played with a small plectrum as well as with the fingers.

The Assyrian trumpet was very similar to **the** Egyptian. Furthermore, we meet with three kinds of drums, of which one is especially noteworthy **on** account of its odd shape, somewhat resembling a sugar-loaf; with the tambourine; with two kinds of cymbals; and with bells, of **which** a considerable number have been found in the mound of Nimroud. These bells, which have greatly withstood the devastation **of time, are** but small in size, the largest of them being only $3\frac{1}{4}$ **inches in** height and $2\frac{1}{2}$ inches in diameter. **Most of** them **have a hole at the** top, in which probably the clapper was fastened. **They are** made of copper mixed with 14 per cent. of tin.

Instrumental music was **used** by **the** Assyrians and Babylonians in their religious observances. This is obvious from the sculptures, and is **to some extent** confirmed by the mode of worship paid by command of king Nebuchadnezzar to the golden image: " Then an herald **cried** aloud, To you it is commanded, O people, nations, and languages, that at what time ye hear **the** sound of the cornet, flute, harp, **sackbut, psaltery, dulcimer, and all** kinds of musick, ye **fall** down **and worship the golden** image that Nebuchadnezzar **the** king hath **set up**." The kings appear to have maintained at their courts musical bands, whose office it was to perform secular music at certain times of the day or on fixed occasions. Of king Darius we are told that, when he had cast Daniel into the den **of** lions, he "went to **his** palace, and passed the night **fasting,** neither were instruments of musick brought **before** him;" from **which** we may conclude that his band was in the habit of playing before him in the evening. A similar custom prevailed also at the court of Jerusalem, at least in the time of David and Solomon; both of whom appear to have had their royal private bands, besides a large number of singers and instrumental performers of sacred music who were engaged in the Temple.

THE HEBREWS.

As regards the musical instruments of the Hebrews, we are from biblical records acquainted with the names of many of them; but representations to be trusted are still wanting, and it is chiefly from an examination of the ancient Egyptian and Assyrian instruments that we can conjecture almost to a certainty their construction and capabilities. From various indications, which it would be too circumstantial here to point out, we believe the Hebrews to have possessed the following instruments:

THE HARP. There cannot be a doubt that the Hebrews possessed the harp, seeing that it was a common instrument among the Egyptians and Assyrians. But it is uncertain which of the Hebrew names of the stringed instruments occurring in the Bible really designates the harp.

THE DULCIMER. Some writers on Hebrew music consider the *nebel* to have been a kind of dulcimer; others conjecture the same of the *psanterin* mentioned in the book of Daniel,—a name which appears to be synonymous with the *psalterion* of the Greeks, and from which also the present oriental dulcimer, *santir*, may have been derived. Some of the instruments mentioned in the book of Daniel may have been synonymous with some which occur in other parts of the Bible under Hebrew names; the names given in Daniel being Chaldæan. The *asor* was a ten-stringed instrument played with a plectrum, and is supposed to have borne some resemblance to the *nebel*.

THE LYRE. This instrument is represented on some Hebrew coins generally ascribed to Judas Maccabæus, who lived in the second century before the Christian era. There are several of them in the British museum; some are of silver, and the others of copper. On three of them are lyres with three strings, another has one with five, and another one with six strings. The two sides of the frame appear to have been made of the horns of animals, or they may have been of wood formed in imitation of two horns which originally were used. Lyres thus constructed are still found in Abyssinia. The Hebrew square-shaped lyre of the time of Simon Maccabæus is probably identical with the *psalterion*. The *kinnor*, the favourite instrument of king David, was most likely a lyre if not a small triangular harp. The lyre was evidently an universally known and favoured instrument among ancient eastern nations. Being more simple in construction than most other stringed instruments it undoubtedly preceded them in antiquity. The *kinnor* is mentioned in the Bible as the oldest stringed instrument, and as the invention of Jubal. Even if the name of one particular stringed instrument is here used for stringed instruments in general, which may possibly be the case, it is only reasonable to suppose that the oldest and most universally known stringed instrument would be mentioned as a representative of the whole class rather than any other. Besides, the *kinnor* was a light and easily portable instrument; king David, according to the Rabbinic records, used to suspend it during the night over his pillow. All its uses mentioned in the Bible are especially applicable to the lyre. And the resemblance of the word *kinnor* to *kithara*, *kissar*, and similar names known to denote the lyre, also tends to confirm the supposition that it refers to this instrument. It is, however, not likely that the instruments of the Hebrews—indeed their music altogether—should have remained entirely unchanged during a period of many centuries. Some modifications were likely to occur even from accidental causes; such, for instance, as the influence of neighbouring nations when the Hebrews came into closer contact with them. Thus may be explained why the accounts of the Hebrew instruments given by Josephus, who lived in the first century of the

MUSICAL INSTRUMENTS.

Christian era, are not in exact accordance with those in the Bible. The lyres at the time of Simon Maccabæus may probably be different from those which were in use about a thousand years earlier, or at the time of David and Solomon when the art of music with the Hebrews was at its zenith.

There appears to be a probability that a Hebrew lyre of the time of Joseph (about 1700 B.C.) is represented on an ancient Egyptian painting discovered in a tomb at Beni Hassan,—which is the name of certain grottoes on the eastern bank of the Nile. Sir Gardner Wilkinson, in his "Manners and Customs of the Ancient Egyptians," observes: "If, when we become better acquainted with the interpretation of hieroglyphics, the 'Strangers' at Beni Hassan should prove to be the arrival of Jacob's family in Egypt, we may examine the Jewish lyre drawn by an Egyptian artist. That this event took place about the period when the inmate of the tomb lived is highly probable—at least, if I am correct in considering Osirtasen I. to be the Pharaoh the patron of Joseph; and it remains for us to decide whether the disagreement in the number of persons here introduced—thirty-seven being written over them in hieroglyphics—is a sufficient objection to their identity. It will not be foreign to the present subject to introduce those figures which are curious, if only considered as illustrative of ancient customs at that early period, and which will be looked upon with unbounded interest should they ever be found to refer to the Jews. The first figure is an Egyptian scribe, who presents an account of their arrival to a person seated, the owner of the tomb, and one of the principal officers of the reigning Pharaoh. The next, also an Egyptian, ushers them into his presence; and two advance bringing presents, the wild goat or ibex and the gazelle, the productions of their country. Four men, carrying bows and clubs, follow, leading an ass on which two children are placed in panniers, accompanied by a boy and four women; and, last of all, another ass laden, and two men—one holding a bow and club, the other a lyre, which he plays with a plectrum. All the men have beards, contrary to the custom of the Egyptians, but very general in the East at that period, and noticed as a peculiarity of foreign uncivilized nations throughout their sculptures. The men have sandals, the women a sort of boot reaching to the ankle—both which were worn by many Asiatic people. The lyre is rude, and differs in form from those generally used in Egypt." In the engraving the lyre-player, another man, and some strange animals from this group, are represented.

THE TAMBOURA. *Minnim, machalath,* and *nebei* are usually supposed to be the names of instruments of the lute or guitar kind. *Minnim,* however, appears more likely to imply stringed instruments in general than any particular instrument.

THE SINGLE PIPE. *Chalil* and *nekeb* were the names of the Hebrew pipes or flutes.

THE DOUBLE PIPE. Probably the *mishrokitha* mentioned in Daniel. The *mishrokitha* is represented in the drawings of our histories of music as a small organ, consisting of seven pipes placed in a box with a mouthpiece for blowing. But the shape of the pipes and of the box as well as the row of keys for the fingers exhibited in the representation of the *mishrokitha* have too much of the European type not to suggest that they are probably a product of the imagination. Respecting the illustrations of Hebrew instruments which usually accompany historical treatises on music and commentaries on the Bible, it ought to be borne in mind that most of them are merely the offspring of conjectures founded on some obscure hints in the Bible, or vague accounts by the Rabbins.

THE SYRINX OR PANDEAN PIPE. Probably the *ugab*, which in the English authorized version of the Bible is rendered "organ."

THE BAGPIPE. The word *sumphonia*, which occurs in the book of Daniel, is, by Forkel and others, supposed to denote a bagpipe. It is remarkable that at the present day the bagpipe is called by the Italian peasantry Zampogna. Another Hebrew instrument, the *magrepha*, generally described as an organ, was more likely only a kind of bagpipe. The *magrepha* is not mentioned in the Bible but is described in the Talmud. In tract Erachin it is recorded to have been a powerful organ which stood in the temple at Jerusalem, and consisted of a case or wind-chest, with ten holes, containing ten pipes. Each pipe was capable of emitting ten different sounds, by means of finger-holes or some similar contrivance: thus one hundred different sounds could be produced on this instrument. Further, the *magrepha* is said to have been provided with two pairs of bellows and with ten keys, by means of which it was played with the fingers. Its tone was, according to the Rabbinic accounts, so loud that it could be heard at an incredibly long distance from the temple. Authorities so widely differ that we must leave it uncertain whether the much-lauded *magrepha* was a bagpipe, an organ, or a kettle-drum. Of the real nature of the Hebrew bagpipe perhaps some idea may be formed from a syrinx with bellows, which has been found represented on one of the ancient terra-cottas excavated in Tarsus, Asia-minor, some years since, and here engraved. These

remains are believed to be about 2000 years old, judging from the figures upon them, and from some coins struck about 200 years B.C. having been found embedded with them. We have therefore before us, probably, the oldest representation of a bag-pipe hitherto discovered.

THE TRUMPET. Three kinds are mentioned in the Bible, viz. the *keren*, the *shophar*, and the *chatzozerah*. The first two were more or less curved and might properly be considered as horns. Most commentators are of opinion that the *keren*—made of ram's horn—was almost identical with the *shophar*, the only difference being that the latter was more curved than the former. The *shophar* is especially remarkable as being the only Hebrew musical instrument which has been preserved to the present day in the religious services of the Jews. It is still blown in the synagogue, as in time of old, at the Jewish new-year's festival, according to the command of Moses (Numb. xxix. 1). The *chatzozerah* was a straight trumpet, about two feet in length, and was sometimes made of silver. Two of these straight trumpets are shown in the famous triumphal procession after the fall of Jerusalem on the arch of Titus, engraved on the next page.

THE DRUM. There can be no doubt that the Hebrews had several kinds of drums. We know, however, only of the *toph*, which appears to have been a tambourine or a small hand-drum like the Egyptian darabouka. In the English version of the Bible the word is rendered *timbrel* or *tabret*. This instrument was especially used in processions on occasions of rejoicing, and also frequently by females. We find it in the hands of Miriam, when she was celebrating with the Israelitish women in songs of joy the destruction of Pharaoh's host; and in the hands of Jephtha's daughter, when she went out to welcome her father. There exists at the present day in the East a small hand-drum called *doff, diff,* or *adufe*—a name which appears to be synonymous with the Hebrew *toph*.

THE SISTRUM. Winer, Saalfchütz, and several other commentators are of opinion that the *menaaneim*, mentioned in 2 Sam. vi.

5, denotes the sistrum. In the English Bible the original is translated *cymbals*.

CYMBALS. The *tzeltzelim*, *metzilloth*, and *metzilthaim*, appear to have been cymbals or similar metallic instruments of percussion, differing in shape and sound.

BELLS. The little bells on the vestments of the high-priest were called *phaamon*. Small golden bells were attached to the lower part of the robes of the high-priest in his sacred ministrations. The Jews have, at the present day, in their synagogues small bells fastened to the rolls of the Law containing the Pentateuch: a kind of ornamentation which is supposed to have been in use from time immemorial.

Besides the names of Hebrew instruments already given there occur several others in the Old Testament, upon the real meaning of which much diversity of opinion prevails. *Jobel* is by some commentators classed with the trumpets, but it is by others believed to designate a loud and cheerful blast of the trumpet, used on particular occasions. If *Jobel* (from which *jubilare* is supposed to be derived) is identical with the name *Jubal*, the inventor of musical instruments, it would appear that the Hebrews appreciated pre-eminently the exhilarating power of music. *Shalishim* is supposed to denote a triangle. *Nechiloth, gittith,* and *machalath,* which occur in the headings of some psalms, are also by commentators supposed to be musical instruments. *Nechiloth* is said to have been a flute, and *gittith* and *machalath* to have been stringed instruments, and *machol* a kind of flute. Again, others maintain that the words denote peculiar modes of performance or certain favourite melodies to which the psalms were directed to be sung, or chanted. According to the records of the Rabbins, the Hebrews in the time of David and Solomon possessed thirty-six different musical instruments. In the Bible only about half that number are mentioned.

Most nations of antiquity ascribed the invention of their musical instruments to their gods, or to certain superhuman beings. The Hebrews attributed it to man; Jubal is mentioned in Genesis as "the father of all such as handle the harp and organ" (*i.e.*, performers on stringed instruments and wind instruments). As instruments of percussion are almost invariably in use long before people are led to construct stringed and wind instruments it might perhaps be surmised that Jubal was not regarded as the inventor of all the Hebrew instruments, but rather as the first professional cultivator of instrumental music.

CHAPTER IV.

THE GREEKS.

MANY musical instruments of the ancient Greeks are known to us by name; but respecting their exact construction and capabilities there still prevails almost as much diversity of opinion as is the case with those of the Hebrews.

It is generally believed that the Greeks derived their musical system from the Egyptians. Pythagoras and other philosophers are said to have studied music in Egypt. It would, however, appear that the Egyptian influence upon Greece, as far as regards this art, has been overrated. Not only have the more perfect Egyptian instruments—such as the larger harps, the tamboura—never been much in favour with the Greeks, but almost all the stringed instruments which the Greeks possessed are stated to have been originally derived from Asia. Strabo says: "Those who regard the whole of Asia, as far as India, as consecrated to Bacchus, point to that country as the origin of a great portion of the present music. One author speaks of 'striking forcibly the Asiatic kithara,' another calls the pipes Berecynthian and Phrygian. Some of the instruments also have foreign names, as Nabla, Sambuka, Barbiton, Magadis, and many others."

We know at present little more of these instruments than that they were in use in Greece. Of the Magadis it is even not satisfactorily ascertained whether it was a stringed or a wind instrument. The other three are known to have been stringed instruments. But they cannot have been anything like such universal favourites as the lyre, because this instrument and perhaps the *trigonon* are almost the only stringed instruments represented in the Greek paintings on pottery and other monumental records. If, as might perhaps be suggested, their taste for beauty of form induced the Greeks to represent the elegant lyre in preference to other stringed instruments, we might at least expect to meet with the harp; an instrument which equals if it does not surpass the lyre in elegance of form.

The representation of Polyhymnia with a harp, depicted on a

splendid Greek vase now in the Munich museum, may be noted as an exceptional instance. This valuable relic dates from the time of Alexander the great. The instrument resembles in construction as well as in shape the Assyrian harp, and has thirteen strings. Polyhymnia is touching them with both hands, using the right hand for the treble and the left for the bass. She is seated, holding the instrument in her lap. Even the little tuning-pegs, which in number are not in accordance with the strings, are placed on the sound-board at the upper part of the frame, exactly as on the Assyrian harp. If then we have here the Greek harp, it was more likely an importation from Asia than from Egypt. In short, as far as can be ascertained, the most complete of the Greek instruments appear to be of Asiatic origin. Especially from the nations who inhabited Asia-minor the Greeks are stated to have adopted several of the most popular. Thus we may read of the short and shrill-sounding pipes of the Carians; of the Phrygian pastoral flute, consisting of several tubes united; of the three-stringed *kithara* of the Lydians; and so on.

The Greeks called the harp *kinyra*, and this may be the reason why in the English translation of the Bible the *kinnor* of the Hebrews, the favourite instrument of king David, is rendered *harp*.

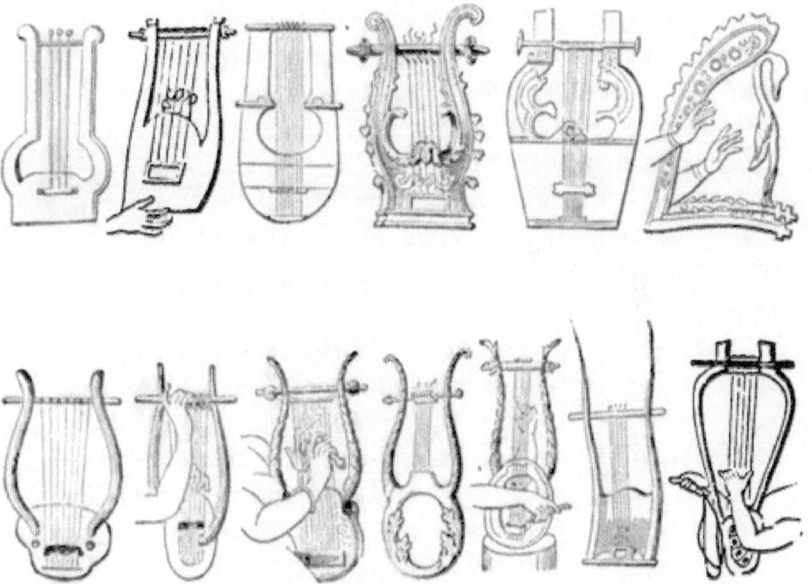

The Greeks had lyres of various kinds, shown in the accompanying woodcuts, more or less differing in construction, form, and size, and distinguished by different names; such as *lyra*, *kithara*, *chelys*, *phorminx*, etc. *Lyra* appears to have implied instruments of this class in general, and also the lyre with a body oval at the base and held upon the lap or in the arms of the performer; while the *kithara* had a square base and was held against the breast. These distinctions have, however, not been satisfactorily ascertained. The *chelys* was a small lyre with the body made of the shell of a tortoise, or of wood in imitation of the tortoise. The *phorminx* was a large lyre; and, like the *kithara*, was used at an early period singly, for accompanying recitations. It is recorded that the *kithara* was employed for solo performances as early as B.C. 700.

The design on the Grecian vase at Munich (already alluded to) represents the nine muses, of whom three are given in the engraving, viz., Polyhymnia with the harp, and Kalliope and Erato with lyres. It will be observed that some of the lyres engraved in the woodcuts on page 29 are provided with a bridge, while others are without it. The largest were held probably on or between the knees, or were attached to the left arm by means of a band, to enable the performer to use his hands without impediment. The strings, made of catgut or sinew, were more usually twanged with a *plektron* than merely with the fingers. The *plektron* was a short stem of ivory or metal pointed at both ends.

A fragment of a Greek lyre which was found in a tomb near Athens is deposited in the British museum. The two pieces constituting its frame are of wood. Their length is about eighteen inches, and the length of the cross-bar at the top is about nine inches. The instrument is unhappily in a condition too dilapidated and imperfect to be of any essential use to the musical inquirer.

The *trigonon* consisted originally of an angular frame, to which the strings were affixed. In the course of time a third bar was added to resist the tension of the strings, and its triangular frame resembled in shape the Greek delta. Subsequently it was still further improved, the upper bar of the frame being made slightly curved, whereby the instrument obtained greater strength and more elegance of form.

The *magadis*, also called *pektis*, had twenty strings which were tuned in octaves, and therefore produced only ten tones. It appears to have been some sort of dulcimer, but information respecting its construction is still wanting. There appears to have been also a kind of bagpipe in use called *magadis*, of which nothing certain is known. Possibly, the same name may have been applied to two different instruments.

The *barbiton* was likewise a stringed instrument of this kind. The *sambyke* is traditionally said to have been invented by Ibykos, B.C. 540. The *simmikon* had thirty-five strings, and derived its name from its inventor, Simos, who lived about B.C. 600. It was perhaps a kind of dulcimer. The *nabla* had only two strings, and probably resembled the *nebel* of the Hebrews, of which but little is known with certainty. The *pandoura* is supposed to have been a kind of lute with three strings. Several of the instruments just noticed were used in Greece, chiefly by musicians who had immigrated from Asia; they can therefore hardly be considered as national musical instruments of the Greeks. The *monochord* had (as its name implies) only a single string, and was used in teaching singing and the laws of acoustics.

The flute, *aulos*, of which there were many varieties, as shown in the woodcut p. 31, was a highly popular instrument, and differed in construction from the flutes and pipes of the ancient Egyptians. Instead of being blown through a hole at the side near the top it

was held like a flageolet, and a vibrating reed was inserted into the mouth-piece, so that it might be more properly described as a kind of oboe or clarionet. The Greeks were accustomed to designate by the name of *aulos* all wind instruments of the flute and oboe kind, some of which were constructed like the flageolet or like our antiquated *flûte à bec*. The single flute was called *monaulos*, and the double one *diaulos*. A *diaulos*, which was found in a tomb at Athens, is in the British museum. The wood of which it is made seems to be cedar, and the tubes are fifteen inches in length. Each tube has a separate mouth-piece and six finger-holes, five of which are at the upper side and one is underneath.

The *syrinx*, or Pandean pipe, had from three to nine tubes, but seven was the usual number. The straight trumpet, *salpinx*, and the curved horn, *keras*, made of brass, were used exclusively in war. The small hand-drum, called *tympanon*, resembled in shape our tambourine, but was covered with parchment at the back as well as at the front. The *kymbala* were made of metal, and resembled our small cymbals. The *krotala* were almost identical with our castanets, and were made of wood or metal.

The Etruscans and Romans.

The Romans are recorded to have derived some of their most popular instruments originally from the Etruscans; a people which at an early period excelled all other Italian nations in the cultivation of the arts as well as in social refinement, and which possessed musical instruments similar to those of the Greeks. It must, however, be remembered that many of the vases and other specimens of art which have been found in Etruscan tombs, and on which delineations of lyres and other instruments occur, are supposed to be productions of Greek artists whose works were obtained from Greece by the Etruscans, or who were induced to settle in Etruria.

The flutes of the Etruscans were not unfrequently made of ivory; those used in religious sacrifices were of box-wood, of a species of the lotus, of ass' bone, bronze and silver. A bronze flute, somewhat resembling our flageolet, has been found in a tomb; likewise a huge trumpet of bronze. An Etruscan *cornu* (engraved) is deposited in the British museum, and measures about four feet in length.

To the Etruscans is also attributed by some the invention of the hydraulic organ. The Greeks possessed a somewhat similar contrivance which they called *hydraulos, i.e.* waterflute, and which probably was identical with the

organum hydraulicum of the Romans. The instrument ought more properly to be regarded as a pneumatic organ, for the sound was produced by the current of air through the pipes; the water applied serving merely to give the necessary pressure to the bellows and to regulate their action. The pipes were probably caused to sound by means of stops, perhaps resembling those on our organ, which were drawn out or pushed in. The construction was evidently but a primitive contrivance, contained in a case which could be carried by one or two persons and which was placed on a table. The highest degree of perfection which the hydraulic organ obtained with the ancients is perhaps

shown in a representation on a coin of the emperor Nero, in the British museum. Only ten pipes are given to it and there is no indication of any key board, which would probably have been shown had it existed. The man standing at the side and holding a laurel leaf in his hand is surmised to represent a victor in the exhibitions of the circus or the amphitheatre. The hydraulic organ probably was played on such occasions; and the medal containing an impression of it may have been bestowed upon the victor.

During the time of the republic, and especially subsequently under the reign of the emperors, the Romans adopted many new instruments from Greece, Egypt, and even from western Asia; without essentially improving any of their importations.

Their most favourite stringed instrument was the lyre, of which they had various kinds, called, according to their form and arrangement of strings, *lyra, cithara, chelys, testudo, fidis* (or *fides*), and *cornu*. The name *cornu* was given to the lyre when the sides of the frame terminated at the top in the shape of two horns. The *barbitos* was a kind of lyre with a large body, which gave the instrument somewhat the shape of the Welsh *crwth*. The

MUSICAL INSTRUMENTS.

psalterium was a kind of lyre of an oblong square shape. Like most of the Roman lyres, it was played with a rather large plectrum. The *trigonum* was the same as the Greek *trigonon*, and was probably originally derived from Egypt. It is recorded that a certain musician of the name of Alexander Alexandrinus was so admirable a performer upon it that when exhibiting his skill in Rome he created the greatest *furore*. Less common, and derived from Asia, were the *sambuca* and *nablia*, the exact construction of which is unknown.

The flute, *tibia*, was originally made of the shin bone, and had a mouth-hole and four finger-holes. Its shape was retained even when, at a later period, it was constructed of other substances than bone. The *tibia gingrina* consisted of a long and thin tube of reed with a mouth-hole at the side of one end. The *tibia obliqua* and *tibia vasca* were provided with mouth-pieces affixed at a right angle to the tube; a contrivance somewhat similar to that on our bassoon. The *tibia longa* was especially used in religious worship. The *tibia curva* was curved at its broadest end. The *tibia ligula* appears to have resembled our flageolet. The *calamus* was nothing more than a simple pipe cut off the kind of reed which the ancients used as a pen for writing.

The Romans had double flutes as well as single flutes. The double flute consisted of two tubes united, either so as to have a mouth-piece in common or to have each a separate mouth-piece. If the tubes were exactly alike the double flute was called *Tibiæ pares*; if they were different from each other, *Tibiæ impares*. Little plugs, or stoppers, were inserted into the finger-holes to regulate the order of intervals. The *tibia* was made in various shapes. The *tibia dextra* was usually constructed of the upper and thinner part of a reed; and the *tibia sinistra*, of the lower and broader part. The performers used also the *capistrum*,—a bandage round the cheeks identical with the *phorbeia* of the Greeks.

The British museum contains a mosaic figure of a Roman girl

playing the *tibia*, which is stated to have been disinterred in the year 1823 on the Via Appia. Here the *holmos* or mouth-piece,

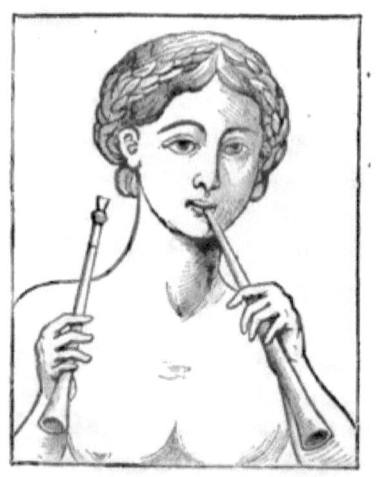

somewhat resembling the reed of our oboe, is distinctly shown. The finger-holes, probably four, are not indicated, although they undoubtedly existed on the instrument.

Furthermore, the Romans had two kinds of Pandean pipes, viz. the *syrinx* and the *fistula*. The bagpipe, *tibia utricularis*, is said to have been a favourite instrument of the emperor Nero.

The *cornu* was a large horn of bronze, curved. The performer held it under his arm with the broad end upwards over his

shoulder. It is represented in the engraving, with the *tuba* and the *lituus*.

The *tuba* was a straight trumpet. Both the *cornu* and the *tuba* were employed in war to convey signals. The same was the case with the *buccina*,—originally perhaps a conch shell, and afterwards a simple horn of an animal,—and the *lituus*, which was bent at the broad end but otherwise straight. The *tympanum* resembled the tambourine and was beaten like the latter with the hands. Among the

Roman instruments of percussion the *scabillum*, which consisted of two plates combined by means of a sort of hinge, deserves to be noticed; it was fastened under the foot and trodden in time, to produce certain rhythmical effects in musical performances. The *cymbalum* consisted of two metal plates similar to our cymbals. The *crotala* and the *crusmata* were kinds of castanets, the former being oblong and of a larger size than the latter. The Romans had also a *triangulum*, which resembled the triangle occasionally used in our orchestra. The *sistrum* they derived from Egypt with the introduction of the worship of Isis. Metal bells, arranged according to a regular order of intervals and placed in a frame, were called *tintinnabula*. The *crepitaculum* appears to have been a somewhat similar contrivance on a hoop with a handle.

Through the Greeks and Romans we have the first well-authenticated proof of musical instruments having been introduced into Europe from Asia. The Romans in their conquests undoubtedly made their musical instruments known, to some extent, also in western Europe. But the Greeks and Romans are not the only nations which introduced eastern instruments into Europe. The Phœnicians at an early period colonized Sardinia, and traces of them are still to be found on that island. Among these is a peculiarly constructed double-pipe, called *lionedda* or *launedda*. Again, at a much later period the Arabs introduced several of their instruments into Spain, from which country they became known in France, Germany, and England. Also the crusaders, during the eleventh and twelfth centuries, may have helped to familiarize the western European nations with instruments of the east.

CHAPTER V.

THE CHINESE.

ALLOWING for any exaggeration as to chronology, natural to the lively imagination of Asiatics, there is no reason to doubt that the Chinese possessed long before our Christian era musical instruments to which they attribute a fabulously high antiquity. There is an ancient tradition, according to which they obtained their musical scale from a miraculous bird, called foung-hoang, which appears to have been a sort of phœnix. When Confucius, who lived about B.C. 500, happened to hear on a certain occasion some Chinese music, he became so greatly enraptured that he could not take any food for three months afterwards. The sounds which produced this effect were those of Kouei, the Orpheus of the Chinese, whose performance on the *king*—a kind of harmonicon constructed of slabs of sonorous stone—would draw wild animals around him and make them subservient to his will. As regards the invention of musical instruments the Chinese have other traditions. In one of these we are told that the origin of some of their most popular instruments dates from the period when China was under the dominion of heavenly spirits, called Ki. Another assigns the invention of several stringed instruments to the great Fohi who was the founder of the empire and who lived about B.C. 3000, which was long after the dominion of the Ki, or spirits. Again, another tradition holds that the most important instruments and systematic arrangements of sounds are an invention of Niuva, a supernatural female, who lived at the time of Fohi.

MUSICAL INSTRUMENTS. 39

According to their records, the Chinese possessed their much-esteemed *king* 2200 years before our Christian era, and employed it for accompanying songs of praise. It was regarded as a sacred instrument. During religious observances at the solemn moment when the *king* was sounded sticks of incense were burnt. It was likewise played before the emperor early in the morning when he awoke. The Chinese have long since constructed

various kinds of the *king*, one of which is here engraved, by using different species of stones. Their most famous stone selected for this purpose is called *yu*. It is not only very sonorous but also beautiful in appearance. The *yu* is found in mountain streams and crevices of rocks. The largest specimens found measure from two to three feet in diameter, but of this size examples rarely occur. The *yu* is very hard and heavy.

Some European mineralogists, to whom the missionaries transmitted specimens for examination, pronounce it to be a species of agate. It is found of different colours, and the Chinese appear to have preferred in different centuries particular colours for the *king*.

The Chinese consider the *yu* especially valuable for musical purposes, because it always retains exactly the same pitch. All other musical instruments, they say, are in this respect doubtful; but the tone of the *yu* is neither influenced by cold nor heat, nor by humidity, nor dryness.

The stones used for the *king* have been cut from time to time in various grotesque shapes. Some represent animals: as, for instance, a bat with outstretched wings; or two fishes placed side by side: others are in the shape of an ancient Chinese bell. The angular shape shown in the engraving appears to be the oldest and is still retained in the ornamented stones of the *pien-king*, which is a more modern instrument than the *king*. The tones of the *pien-king* are attuned according to the Chinese intervals called *lu*, of which there are twelve in the compass of an octave. The same is the case with the other Chinese instruments of this class. They vary, however, in pitch. The pitch of the *soung-king*, for instance, is four intervals lower than that of the *pien-king*.

Sonorous stones have always been used by the Chinese also singly, as rhythmical instruments. Such a single stone is called *tse-king*. Probably certain curious relics belonging to a temple in Peking, erected for the worship of Confucius, serve a similar purpose. In one of the outbuildings of the temple are ten sonorous stones, shaped like drums, which are asserted to have been cut about three thousand years ago. The primitive Chinese characters engraven upon them are nearly obliterated.

The ancient Chinese had several kinds of bells, frequently arranged in sets so as to constitute a musical scale. The Chinese name for the bell is *tchung*. At an early period they had a somewhat square-shaped bell called *té tchung*. Like other ancient Chinese bells it was made of copper alloyed with tin, the proportion being one pound of tin to six of copper. The *té-tchung*, which is also known by the name of *piao*, was principally used to indicate the time and divisions in musical performances. It had a fixed pitch of sound, and several of these bells attuned to a certain order of intervals were not unfrequently ranged in a regular succession, thus forming a musical instrument

which was called *pien-tchung*. The musical scale of the sixteen bells which the *pien-tchung* contained was the same as that of the *king* before mentioned.

The *hiuen-tchung* was, according to popular tradition, included with the antique instruments at the time of Confucius, and came into popular use during the Han dynasty (from B.C. 200 until A.D. 200). It was of a peculiar oval shape and had nearly the same quaint ornamentation as the *té-tchung;* this consisted of symbolical figures, in four divisions, each containing nine mammals. The mouth was crescent-shaped. Every figure had a deep meaning referring to the seasons and to the mysteries of the Buddhist religion. The largest *hiuen-tchung* was about twenty inches in length; and, like the *té-tchung*, was sounded by means of a small wooden mallet with an oval knob. None of the bells of this description had a clapper. It would, however, appear that the Chinese had at an early period some kind of bell provided with a wooden tongue: this was used for military purposes as well as for calling the people together when an imperial messenger promulgated his sovereign's commands. An expression of Confucius is recorded to the effect that he wished to be "A wooden-tongued bell of Heaven," *i.e.* a herald of heaven to proclaim the divine purposes to the multitude.

The *fang-hiang* was a kind of wood-harmonicon. It contained sixteen wooden slabs of an oblong square shape, suspended in a wooden frame elegantly decorated. The slabs were arranged in two tiers, one above the other, and were all of equal length and breadth but differed in thickness. The *tchoung-tou* consisted of twelve slips of bamboo, and was used for beating time and for rhythmical purposes. The slips being banded together at one end could be expanded somewhat like a fan. The Chinese state that they used the *tchoung-tou* for writing upon before they invented paper.

The *ou*, of which we give a woodcut, likewise an ancient Chinese instrument of percussion and still in use, is made of wood in the shape of a crouching tiger. It is hollow, and along its back are about twenty small pieces of metal, pointed, and in appearance not unlike the teeth of a saw. The performer strikes them with a sort of plectrum resembling a brush, or with a small stick called *tchen*.

Occasionally the *ou* is made with pieces of metal shaped like reeds.

The ancient *ou* was constructed with only six tones which were attuned thus—

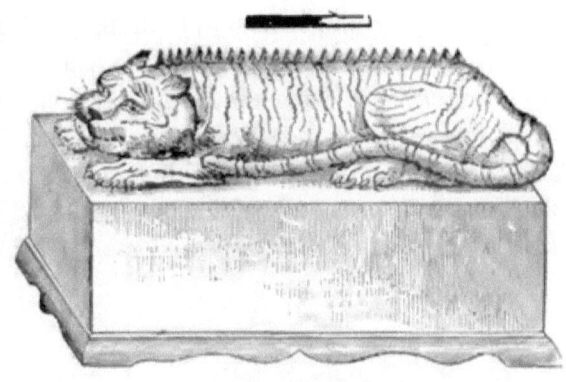

f, g, a c, d, f. The instrument appears to have become deteriorated in the course of time; for, although it has gradually acquired as many as twenty-seven pieces of metal, it evidently serves at the present day more for the production of rhythmical noise than for the execution of any melody. The modern *ou* is made of a species of wood called *kieou* or *tsieou*: and the tiger rests generally on a hollow wooden pedestal about three feet six inches long, which serves as a sound-board.

The *tchou*, likewise an instrument of percussion, was made of the wood of a tree called *kieou-mou*, the stem of which resembles that of the pine and whose foliage is much like that of the cypress. It was constructed of boards about three-quarters of an inch in thickness. In the middle of one of the sides was an aperture into which the hand was passed for the purpose of holding the handle of a wooden hammer, the end of which  entered into a hole situated in the bottom of the *tchou*. The handle was kept in its place by means of a wooden pin, on which it moved right and left when the instrument was struck with a hammer. The Chinese ascribe to the *tchou* a very high antiquity, as they almost invariably do with any of their inventions when the date of its origin is unknown to them.

The *po-fou* was a drum, about one foot four inches in length, and seven inches in diameter. It had a parchment at each end, which was prepared in a peculiar way by being boiled in water. The *po-fou* used to be partly filled with a preparation made from the husk of rice, in order to mellow the sound. The Chinese name for the drum is *kou*.

The *kin-kou* (engraved), a large drum fixed on a pedestal which raises it above six feet from the ground, is embellished with symbolical designs. A similar drum on which natural phenomena are depicted is called *lei-kou;* and another of the kind, with figures of certain birds and beasts which are regarded as symbols of long life, is called *ling-kou*, and also *lou-kou*.

The flutes, *ty*, *yo*, and *tché* were generally made of bamboo. The *koan-tsee* was a Pandean pipe containing twelve tubes of bamboo. The *siao*, likewise a Pandean pipe, contained sixteen tubes. The *pai-siao* differed from the *siao* inasmuch as the tubes were inserted into an oddly-shaped case highly ornamented with grotesque designs and silken appendages.

The Chinese are known to have constructed at an early period a curious wind-instrument, called *hiuen*. It was made of baked clay and had five finger-holes, three of which were placed on one side and two on the opposite side, as in the cut. Its tones were in conformity with the pentatonic scale. The reader unacquainted with the pentatonic scale may ascertain its character by playing on the pianoforte the scale of C major with the omission of *f* and *b* (the *fourth* and *seventh*); or by striking the black keys in regular succession from *f*-sharp to the next *f*-sharp above or below.

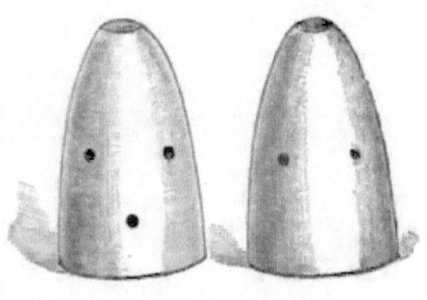

Another curious wind-instrument of high antiquity, the *cheng*, (engraved, p. 46) is still in use. Formerly it had either 13, 19, or 24 tubes, placed in a calabash; and a long curved tube served as a mouth-piece. In olden time it was called *yu*.

The ancient stringed instruments, the *kin* and *ché*, were of the dulcimer kind: they are still in use, and specimens of them are in the South Kensington museum.

The Buddhists introduced from Thibet into China their god of music, who is represented as a rather jovial-looking man with a moustache and an imperial, playing the *pepa*, a kind of lute with four silken strings. Perhaps some interesting information respecting the ancient Chinese musical instruments may be gathered from the famous ruins of the Buddhist temples *Ongcor-Wat* and *Ongcor-Thôm*, in Cambodia. These splendid ruins are supposed to be above two thousand years old; and, at any rate, the circumstance of their age not being known to the Cambodians suggests a high antiquity. On the bas-reliefs with which the temples were enriched are figured musical instruments, which European travellers describe as "flutes, organs, trumpets, and drums, resembling those of the Chinese." Faithful sketches of these representations might, very likely, afford valuable hints to the student of musical history.

THE HINDUS.

In the Brahmin mythology of the Hindus the god Nareda is the inventor of the *vina*, the principal national instrument of Hindustan. Saraswati, the consort of Brahma, may be regarded as the Minerva of the Hindus. She is the goddess of music as well as of speech; to her is attributed the invention of the systematic arrangement of the sounds into a musical scale. She is represented seated on a peacock and playing on a stringed instrument of the lute kind. Brahma himself we find depicted as a vigorous man with four handsome heads, beating with his hands upon a small drum; and Vishnu, in his incarnation as Krishna, is represented as a beautiful youth playing upon a flute. The Hindus construct a peculiar kind of flute, which they consider as the favourite instrument of Krishna. They have also the divinity Ganesa, the god of Wisdom, who is represented as a man with the head of an elephant, holding a *tamboura* in his hands.

It is a suggestive fact that we find among several nations in different parts of the world an ancient tradition, according to which their most popular stringed instrument was originally derived from the water.

In Hindu mythology the god Nareda invented the *vina*—the principal national instrument of Hindustan—which has also the name *cach'-hapi*, signifying a tortoise (*testudo*). Moreover, *nara* denotes in Sanskrit water, and *narada*, or *nareda*, the giver of water. Like Nareda, Nereus and his fifty daughters, the Nereides, were much renowned for their musical accomplishments; and Hermes (it will be remembered) made his lyre, the *chelys*, of a tortoise-shell. The Scandinavian god Odin, the originator of magic songs, is mentioned as the ruler of the sea, and as such he had the name of *Nikarr*. In the depth of the sea he played the harp with his subordinate spirits, who occasionally came up to the surface of the water to teach some favoured human being their wonderful instrument. Wäinämöinen, the divine player on the Finnish *kantele* (according to the Kalewala, the old national epic of the Finns) constructed his instrument of fish-bones. The frame he made out of the bones of the pike; and the teeth of the pike he used for the tuning-pegs.

Jacob Grimm in his work on German mythology points out an old tradition, preserved in Swedish and Scotch national ballads, of a skilful harper who constructs his instrument out of the bones of a young girl drowned by a wicked woman. Her fingers he uses for the tuning screws, and her golden hair for the strings. The harper plays, and his music kills the murderess. A similar story is told in the old Icelandic national songs; and the same tradition has been preserved in the Faroe islands, as well as in Norway and Denmark.

May not the agreeable impression produced by the rhythmical flow of the waves and the soothing murmur of running water have led various nations, independently of each other, to the widespread conception that they obtained their favourite instrument of music from the water? Or is the notion traceable to a common source dating from a pre-historic age, perhaps from the early period when the Aryan race is surmised to have diffused its lore through various countries? Or did it originate in the old belief that the world, with all its charms and delights, arose from a chaos in which water constituted the predominant element?

Howbeit, Nareda, the giver of water, was evidently also the ruler of the clouds; and Odin had his throne in the skies. Indeed, many of the musical water-spirits appear to have been originally considered as rain deities. Their music may therefore be regarded as derived from the clouds rather than from the sea. In short, the traditions respecting spirits and water are not in contradiction to the opinion of the ancient Hindus that music is of heavenly origin, but rather tend to support it.

The earliest musical instruments of the Hindus on record have, almost all of them, remained in popular use until the present day scarcely altered. Besides these, the Hindus possess several Arabic and Persian instruments which are of comparatively modern date in Hindustan: evidently having been introduced into that country scarcely a thousand years ago, at the time of the Mahomedan irruption. There is a treatise on music extant, written in Sanskrit, which contains a description of the ancient instruments. Its title is *Sángita ráthnakara*. If, as may be hoped, it be translated by a Sanskrit scholar who is at the same time a good musician, we shall probably be enabled to ascertain more exactly which of the Hindu instruments of the present day are of comparatively modern origin.

The *vina* is undoubtedly of high antiquity. It has seven wire strings, and movable frets which are generally fastened with wax. Two hollowed gourds, often tastefully ornamented, are affixed to it for the purpose of increasing the sonorousness. There are several kinds of the *vina* in different districts; but that represented in the illustration is regarded as the oldest. The performer shown is Jeewan Shah, a celebrated virtuoso on the *vina*, who lived about a hundred years ago. The Hindus divided their musical scale into several intervals smaller than our modern semitones. They adopted twenty-two intervals called *sruti* in the compass of an octave, which may therefore

be compared to our chromatic intervals. As the frets of the *vina* are movable the performer can easily regulate them according to the scale, or mode, which he requires for his music.

The harp, *chang*, has become almost obsolete. If some Hindu drawings of it can be relied upon, it had at an early time a triangular frame and was in construction as well as in shape and size almost identical with the Assyrian harp.

The Hindus claim to have invented the violin bow. They maintain that the *ravanastron*, one of their old instruments played with the bow, was invented about five thousand years ago by Ravanon, a mighty king of Ceylon. However this may be there is a great probability that the fiddle-bow originated in Hindustan; because Sanskrit scholars inform us that there are names for it in works which cannot be less than from 1500 to 2000 years old. The non-occurrence of any instrument played with a bow on the monuments of the nations of antiquity is by no means so sure a proof as has generally been supposed, that the bow was unknown. The fiddle in its primitive condition must have been a poor **contrivance**. It probably was despised by players who could produce better tones with greater facility by twanging the strings with their fingers, or with a plectrum. Thus it may have **remained** through many centuries without experiencing any **material** improvement. It **must also** be borne in mind that the **monuments** transmitted **to us chiefly** represent historical events, **religious** ceremonies, and **royal entertainments**. On such occasions instruments of a **certain kind only were used, and these we** find **represented; while others,** which may **have been even more** common, **never occur.** In two thousand years' time people will possibly **maintain that some** highly perfected instrument popular with them **was** entirely unknown **to us,** because it is at present in so primitive a condition that no **one** hardly notices it. If the *ravanastron* was an importation of the Mahomedans it would most likely bear some resemblance to the Arabian and Persian instruments, and it would be found rather in the hands of the higher classes in the towns; whereas it is principally met with among the lower order of people, in isolated and mountainous districts. It is further remarkable that the most simple kind of *ravanastron* is almost identical with the Chinese fiddle called *ur-heen*. This species has only two strings, and its **body consists of a small block** of wood, hollowed **out and covered with the skin of a serpent.** The *ur-heen* has not been mentioned among the most ancient instruments of the Chinese, since there is no evidence of its having been known in China before the introduction of the Buddhist religion into that country. From indications, which to point out would lead too far here, it would appear that several instruments found in China originated in Hindustan. They seem to have been gradually diffused from Hindustan and Thibet, more or less altered in the course of time, through the east as far as Japan.

Another curious Hindu instrument, probably of very high antiquity, is the *poongi*, also called *toumrie* and *magoudi*. It consists of a gourd or of the Cuddos nut, hollowed, into which two pipes are inserted. The *poongi* therefore somewhat resembles in appearance a bagpipe. It is generally used by the *Sampuris* or snake charmers, who play upon it when they exhibit the antics of the cobra. The name *magoudi*, given in certain districts to this instrument, rather tends to corroborate the opinion of some musical historians that the *magadis* of the ancient Greeks was a sort of double-pipe, or bagpipe.

Many instruments of Hindustan are known by different names in different districts; and, besides, there are varieties of them. On the whole, the Hindus possess about fifty instruments. To describe them properly would fill a volume. Some, which are in the Kensington museum, will be found noticed in the large catalogue of that collection.

THE PERSIANS AND ARABS.

Of the musical instruments of the ancient Persians, before the Christian era, scarcely anything is known. It may be surmised that they closely resembled those of the Assyrians, and probably also those of the Hebrews.

The harp, *chang*, in olden time a favourite instrument of the Persians, has gradually fallen into desuetude. The illustration of a small harp given in the woodcut has been sketched from the celebrated sculptures, perhaps of the sixth century, which exist on a stupendous rock, called Tackt-i-Bostan, in the vicinity of the town of Kermanshah. These sculptures are said to have been executed during the lifetime of the Persian monarch Khosroo Purviz.

They form the ornaments of two lofty arches, and consist of representations of field sports and aquatic amusements. In one of the boats is seated a man in an ornamental dress, with a halo round his head, who is receiving an arrow from one of his attendants; while a female, who is sitting near him, plays on a Trigonon. Towards the top of the bas-relief is represented a stage, on which are performers on small straight trumpets and little hand drums; six harpers; and four other musicians, apparently females,—the first of whom plays a flute; the second, a sort of pandean pipe; the third, an instrument which is too much defaced to be recognizable; and the fourth, a bagpipe. Two

harps of a peculiar shape were copied by Sir Gore Ousely from Persian manuscripts about four hundred years old resembling, in the principle on which they are constructed, all other oriental harps. There existed evidently various kinds of the *chang*. It may be remarked here that the instrument *tschenk* (or *chang*) in use at the present day in Persia, is more like a dulcimer than a harp. The Arabs adopted the harp from the Persians, and called it *junk*. An interesting representation of a Turkish woman playing the harp (p. 53) sketched from life by Melchior Lorich in the seventeenth century, probably exhibits an old Persian *chang*; for the Turks derived their music principally from Persia. Here we have an introduction into Europe of the oriental frame without a front pillar.

The Persians appear to have adopted, at an early period, smaller musical intervals than semitones. When the Arabs conquered Persia (A.D. 641) the Persians had already attained a higher degree of civilisation than their conquerors. The latter found in Persia the cultivation of music considerably in advance of their own, and the musical instruments superior also. They soon adopted the Persian instruments, and there can be no doubt that the musical system exhibited by the earliest Arab writers whose works on the theory of music have been preserved was based upon an older system of the Persians. In these works the octave is divided in seventeen *one-third-tones*—intervals which are still made use of in the east. Some of the Arabian instruments

are constructed so as to enable the performer to produce the intervals with exactness. The frets on the lute and tamboura, for instance, are regulated with a view to this object.

The Arabs had to some extent become acquainted with many of the Persian instruments before the time of their conquest of Persia. An Arab musician of the name of Nadr Ben el-Hares Ben Kelde is recorded as having been sent to the Persian king Khosroo Purviz, in the sixth century, for the purpose of learning Persian singing and performing on the lute. Through him, it is said, the lute was brought to Mekka. Saib Chatir, the son of a Persian, is spoken of as the first performer on the lute in Medina, A.D. 682; and of an Arab lutist, Ebn Soreidsch from Mekka, A.D. 683, it is especially mentioned that he played in the Persian style; evidently the superior one. The lute, *el-oud*, had before the tenth century only four strings, or four pairs producing four tones, each tone having two strings tuned in unison. About the tenth century a string for a fifth tone was added. The strings were made of silk neatly twisted. The neck of the instrument was provided with frets of string, which were carefully regulated according to the system of seventeen intervals in the compass of an octave before mentioned. Other favourite stringed instruments were the *tamboura*, a kind of lute with a long neck, and the *kanoon*, a kind of dulcimer strung with lamb's gut strings (generally three in unison for each tone) and played upon with two little plectra which the performer had fastened to his fingers. The *kanoon* is likewise still in use in countries inhabited by Mahomedans. The engraving, taken from a Persian painting at Teheran, represents an old Persian *santir*, the prototype of our dulcimer, mounted with wire strings and played upon with two slightly curved sticks.

Al-Farabi, one of the earliest Arabian musical theorists known, who lived in the beginning of the tenth century, does not allude to the fiddle-bow. This is noteworthy inasmuch as it seems in some measure to support the opinion maintained by some historians that the bow originated in England or Wales. Unfortunately we possess no exact descriptions of the Persian and

Arabian instruments between the tenth and fourteenth centuries, otherwise we should probably have earlier accounts of some instrument of the violin kind in Persia. Ash-shakandi, who lived in Spain about A.D. 1200, mentions the *rebab*, which may have been in use for centuries without having been thought worthy of notice on account of its rudeness. Persian writers of the fourteenth century speak of two instruments of the violin class, viz., the *rebab* and the *kemangeh*. As regards the *kemangeh*, the Arabs themselves assert that they obtained it from Persia, and their statement appears all the more worthy of belief from the fact that both names, *rebab* and *kemangeh*, are originally Persian. We engrave the *rebab* from an example at South Kensington.

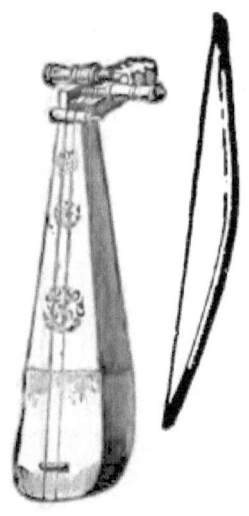

The *nay*, a flute, and the *surnay*, a species of oboe, are still popular in the east.

The Arabs must have been indefatigable constructors of musical instruments. Kiesewetter gives a list of above two hundred names of Arabian instruments, and this does not include many known to us through Spanish historians. A careful investigation of the musical instruments of the Arabs during their sojourn in Spain is particularly interesting to the student of mediæval music, inasmuch as it reveals the eastern origin of many instruments which are generally regarded as European inventions. Introduced into Spain by the Saracens and the Moors they were gradually diffused towards northern Europe. The English, for instance, adopted not only the Moorish dance (morrice dance) but also the *kuitra* (gittern), the *el-oud* (lute), the *rebab* (rebec), the *nakkarah* (naker), and several others. In an old Cornish sacred drama, supposed to date from the fourteenth century, we have in an enumeration of musical instruments the *nakrys*, designating "kettle-drums." It must be remembered that the Cornish language, which has now become obsolete, was nearly akin to the Welsh. Indeed, names of musical instruments derived from the Moors in Spain occur in almost every European language.

Not a few fanciful stories are traditionally preserved among the Arabs testifying to the wonderful effects they ascribed to the power of their instrumental performances. One example will suffice. Al-Farabi had acquired his proficiency in Spain, in one of the schools at Cordova which flourished as early as towards the end of the ninth century: and his reputation became so great that ultimately it extended to Asia. The mighty caliph of Bagdad himself desired to hear the celebrated musician, and sent messengers to Spain with instructions to offer rich presents to him and to convey him to the court. But Al-Farabi feared that if he went he should be retained in Asia, and should never again see the home to which he felt deeply attached. At last he resolved to disguise himself, and ventured to undertake the journey which promised him a rich harvest. Dressed in a mean costume, he made his appearance at the court just at the time when the caliph was being entertained with his daily concert. Al-Farabi, unknown to everyone, was permitted to exhibit his skill on the lute. Scarcely had he commenced his performance in a certain musical mode when he set all his audience laughing aloud, notwithstanding the efforts of the courtiers to suppress so unbecoming an exhibition of mirth in the royal presence. In truth, even the caliph himself was compelled to burst out into a fit of laughter. Presently the performer changed to another mode, and the effect was that immediately all his hearers began to sigh, and soon tears of sadness replaced the previous tears of mirth. Again he played in another mode, which excited his audience to such a rage that they would have fought each other if he, seeing the danger, had not directly gone over to an appeasing mode. After this wonderful exhibition of his skill Al-Farabi concluded in a mode which had the effect of making his listeners fall into a profound sleep, during which he took his departure.

It will be seen that this incident is almost identical with one recorded as having happened about twelve hundred years earlier at the court of Alexander the great, and which forms the subject of Dryden's " Alexander's Feast." The distinguished flutist Timotheus successively aroused and subdued different passions by changing the musical modes during his performance, exactly in the same way as did Al-Farabi.

CHAPTER VI.

THE AMERICAN INDIANS.

If the preserved antiquities of the American Indians, dating from a period anterior to our discovery of the western hemisphere, possess an extraordinary interest because they afford trustworthy evidence of the degree of progress which the aborigines had attained in the cultivation of the arts and in their social condition before they came in contact with Europeans, it must be admitted that the ancient musical instruments of the American Indians are also worthy of examination. Several of them are constructed in a manner which, in some degree, reveals the characteristics of the musical system prevalent among the people who used the instruments. And although most of these interesting relics, which have been obtained from tombs and other hiding-places, may not be of great antiquity, it has been satisfactorily ascertained that they are genuine contrivances of the Indians before they were influenced by European civilization.

Some account of these relics is therefore likely to prove of interest also to the ethnologist, especially as several facts may perhaps be found of assistance in elucidating the still unsolved problem as to the probable original connection of the American with Asiatic races.

Among the instruments of the Aztecs in Mexico and of the Peruvians none have been found so frequently, and have been preserved in their former condition so unaltered, as pipes and flutes. They are generally made of pottery or of bone, substances which are unsuitable for the construction of most other instruments, but which are remarkably well qualified to withstand the decaying influence of time. There is, therefore, no reason to conclude from the frequent occurrence of such instruments that they were more common than other kinds of which specimens have rarely been discovered.

The Mexicans possessed a small whistle formed of baked clay, a considerable number of which have been found. Some specimens (of which we give engravings) are singularly grotesque in

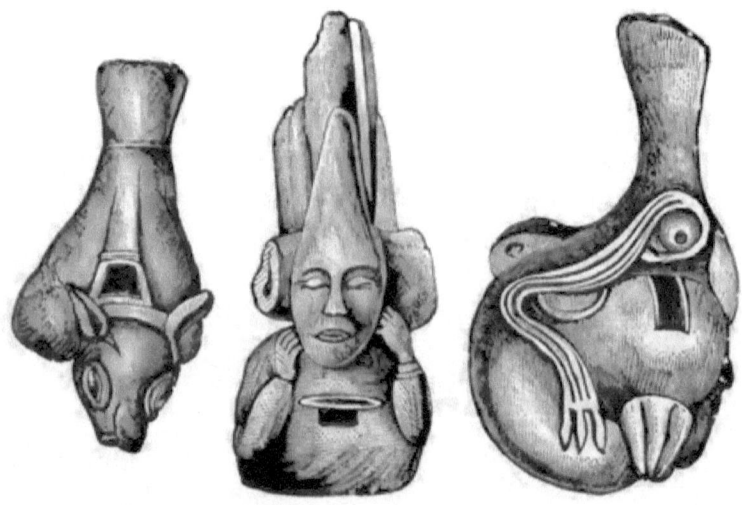

shape, representing caricatures of the human face and figure, birds, beasts, and flowers. Some were provided at the top with a finger-hole which, when closed, altered the pitch of the sound, so that two different tones were producible on the instrument. Others had a little ball of baked clay lying loose inside the air-chamber. When the instrument was blown the current of air set the ball in a vibrating motion, thereby causing a shrill and whirring sound. A similar contrivance is sometimes made use of by Englishmen for conveying signals. The Mexican whistle most likely served principally the same purpose, but it may possibly have been used also in musical entertainments. In the Russian horn band each musician is restricted to a single tone; and similar combinations of performers—only, of course, much more rude—have been witnessed by travellers among some tribes in Africa and America.

Rather more complete than the above specimens are some of the whistles and small pipes which have been found in graves of the Indians of Chiriqui in central America. The pipe or whistle which is represented in the accompanying engraving ap-

pears, to judge from the somewhat obscure description transmitted to us, to possess about half a dozen tones. It is of pottery, painted in red and black on a cream-coloured ground, and in length about five inches. Among the instruments of this kind from central America the most complete have four finger-holes. By means of three the following four sounds (including the sound which is produced when none of the holes are closed) can be emitted:  the fourth finger-hole, when closed, has the effect of lowering the pitch a semitone. By a particular process two or three lower notes are obtainable.

The pipe of the Aztecs, which is called by the Mexican Spaniards *pito*, somewhat resembled our flageolet: the material was a reddish pottery, and it was provided with four finger-holes. Although among about half a dozen specimens which the writer has examined some are considerably larger than others they all have, singularly enough, the same pitch of sound. The smallest is about six inches in length, and the largest about nine inches. Several *pitos* have been found in a remarkably well-preserved condition. They are easy to blow, and their order of intervals is in conformity with the pentatonic scale, thus : The usual shape of the *pito* is that here represented ; showing the upper side of one pipe, and a side view of another. A specimen of a less common shape, also engraved, is in the British museum. Indications

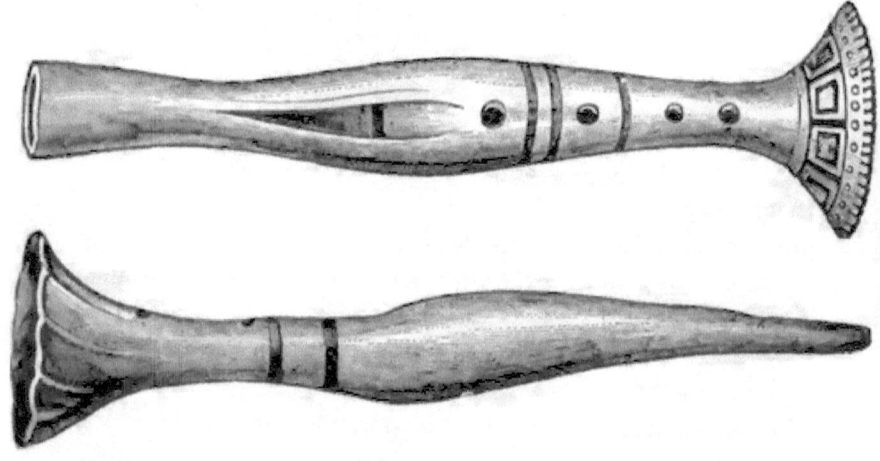

suggestive of the popular estimation in which the flute (or perhaps, more strictly speaking, the pipe) was held by the Aztecs are not wanting. It was played in religious observances and

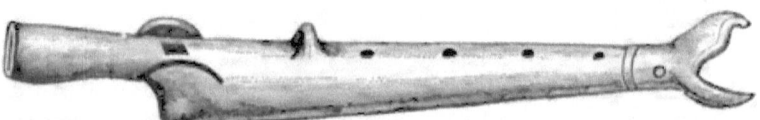

we find it referred to allegorically in orations delivered on solemn occasions. For instance, at the religious festival which was held in honour of Tezcatlepoca—a divinity depicted as a handsome youth, and considered second only to the supreme being—a young man was sacrificed who, in preparation for the ceremony, had been instructed in the art of playing the flute. Twenty days before his death four young girls, named after the principal goddesses, were given to him as companions; and when the hour arrived in which he was to be sacrificed he observed the established symbolical rite of breaking a flute on each of the steps, as he ascended the temple.

Again, at the public ceremonies which took place on the accession of a prince to the throne the new monarch addressed a prayer to the god, in which occurred the following allegorical expression:—"I am thy flute; reveal to me thy will; breathe into me thy breath like into a flute, as thou hast done to my predecessors on the throne. As thou hast opened their eyes, their ears, and their mouth to utter what is good, so likewise do to me. I resign myself entirely to thy guidance." Similar sentences occur in the orations addressed to the monarch. In reading them one can hardly fail to be reminded of Hamlet's reflections addressed to Guildenstern, when the servile courtier expresses his inability to "govern the ventages" of the pipe and to make the instrument "discourse most eloquent music," which the prince bids him to do.

M. de Castelnau in his "Expédition dans l'Amérique" gives among the illustrations of objects discovered in ancient Peruvian tombs a flute made of a human bone. It has four finger-holes at its upper surface and appears to have been blown into at one end. Two bone-flutes, in appearance similar to the engraving given by M. de Castelnau, which have been disinterred at Truxillo are deposited in the British museum. They are about six inches in length, and each is provided with five finger-holes. One of these has all the holes at its upper side, and one of the holes is considerably smaller than the rest. The specimen which we engrave (p. 64) is ornamented with some simple designs in black. The other has four holes at its upper side and one underneath, the latter being placed near to the end at which the instrument evidently was blown. In the aperture of this end some remains

of a hardened paste, or resinous substance, are still preserved. This substance probably was inserted for the purpose of narrowing the end of the tube, in order to facilitate the producing of the sounds. The same contrivance is still resorted to in the construction of the bone-flutes by some Indian tribes in Guiana. The bones of slain enemies appear to have been considered especially appropriate for such flutes. The Araucanians, having killed a prisoner, made flutes of his bones, and danced and "thundered out their dreadful war-songs, accompanied by the mournful sounds of these horrid instruments." Alonso de Ovalle says of the Indians in Chili: "Their flutes, which they play upon in their dances, are made of the bones of the Spaniards and other enemies whom they have overcome in war. This they do by way of triumph and glory for their victory. They make them likewise of bones of animals; but the warriors dance only to the flutes made of their enemies." The Mexicans and Peruvians obviously possessed a great variety of pipes and flutes, some of which are still in use among certain Indian tribes. Those which were found in the famous ruins at Palenque are deposited in the museum in Mexico. They are:—The *cuyvi*, a pipe on which only five tones were producible; the *huayllaca*, a sort of flageolet; the *pincullu*, a flute; and the *chayna*, which is described as "a flute whose lugubrious and melancholy tones filled the heart with indescribable sadness, and brought involuntary tears into the eyes." It was perhaps a kind of oboe.

The Peruvians had the syrinx, which they called *huayra-puhura*. Some clue to the proper meaning of this name may perhaps be gathered from the word *huayra*, which signifies "air." The

MUSICAL INSTRUMENTS.

huayra-puhura was made of cane, and also of stone. Sometimes an embroidery of needle-work was attached to it as an ornament. One specimen which has been disinterred is adorned with twelve figures precisely resembling Maltese crosses. The cross is a figure which may readily be supposed to suggest itself very naturally; and it is therefore not so surprising, as it may appear at a first glance, that the American Indians used it not unfrequently in designs and sculptures before they came in contact with Christians.

The British museum possesses a *huayra-puhura* consisting of fourteen reed pipes of a brownish colour, tied together in two rows by means of thread, so as to form a double set of seven reeds. Both sets are almost exactly of the same dimensions and are placed side by side. The shortest of these reeds measure three inches, and the longest six and a half. In one set they are open at the bottom, and in the other they are closed. Consequently, octaves are produced. The reader is probably aware that the closing of a pipe at the end raises its pitch an octave. Thus, in our organ, the so-called stopped diapason, a set of closed pipes, requires tubes of only half the length of those which constitute the open diapason, although both these stops produce tones in the same pitch; the only difference between them being

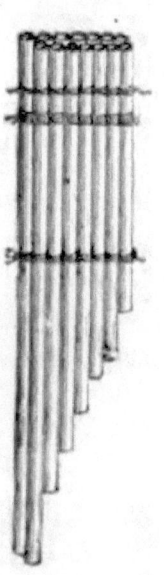

the quality of sound, which in the former is less bright than in the latter.

The tones yielded by the *huayra-puhura* in question are as follows :  The highest octave is

indistinct, owing to some injury done to the shortest tubes; but sufficient evidence remains to show that the intervals were purposely arranged according to the pentatonic scale. This interesting relic was brought to light from a tomb at Arica.

Another *huayra-puhura*, likewise still yielding sounds, was discovered placed over a corpse in a Peruvian tomb, and was procured by the French general, Paroissien. This instrument is made of a greenish stone which is a species of talc, and contains

eight pipes. In the Berlin museum may be seen a good plaster cast taken from this curious relic. The height is 5⅜ inches, and its width 6¼ inches. Four of the tubes have small lateral finger-holes which, when closed, lower the pitch a semitone. These holes are on the second, fourth, six, and seventh pipe, as shown in the engraving. When the holes are open, the tones are:  and when they are closed:

 The other tubes have unalterable tones.

The following notation exhibits all the tones producible on the instrument:

The musician is likely to speculate what could have induced the Peruvians to adopt so strange a series of intervals: it seems rather arbitrary than premeditated.

MUSICAL INSTRUMENTS.

If (and this seems not to be improbable) the Peruvians considered those tones which are produced by closing the lateral holes as additional intervals only, a variety of scales or kinds of *modes* may have been contrived by the admission of one or other of these tones among the essential ones. If we may conjecture from some remarks of Garcilasso de la Vega, and other historians, the Peruvians appear to have used different orders of intervals for different kinds of tunes, in a way similar to what we find to be the case with certain Asiatic nations. We are told for instance "Each poem, or song, had its appropriate tune, and they could not put two different songs to one tune; and this was why the enamoured gallant, making music at night on his flute, with the tune which belonged to it, told the lady and all the world the joy or sorrow of his soul, the favour or ill-will which he possessed; so that it might be said that he spoke by the flute." Thus also the Hindus have certain tunes for certain seasons and fixed occasions, and likewise a number of different modes or scales used for particular kinds of songs.

Trumpets are often mentioned by writers who have recorded the manners and customs of the Indians at the time of the discovery of America. There are, however, scarcely any illustrations to be relied on of these instruments transmitted to us. The Conch was frequently used as a trumpet for conveying signals in war.

The engraving represents a kind of trumpet made of wood, and nearly seven feet in length, which Gumilla found among the

Indians in the vicinity of the Orinoco. It somewhat resembles the *juruparis*, a mysterious instrument of the Indians on the Rio Haupés, a tributary of the Rio Negro, south America. The *juruparis* is regarded as an object of great veneration. Women are never permitted to see it. So stringent is this law that any woman obtaining a sight of it is put to death—usually by poison. No youths are allowed to see it until they have been subjected to a series of initiatory fastings and scourgings. The *juruparis* is usually kept hidden in the bed of some stream, deep in the forest; and no one dares to drink out of that sanctified stream, or to bathe in its water. At feasts the *juruparis* is brought out during the night, and is blown outside the houses of entertainment. The inner portion of the instrument consists of a tube made of slips of the Paxiaba palm (*Triartea exorrhiza*). When the Indians are about to use the instrument they nearly close the upper end of the tube with clay, and also tie above the oblong square hole (shown in the engraving) a portion of the leaf of the Uaruma, one of

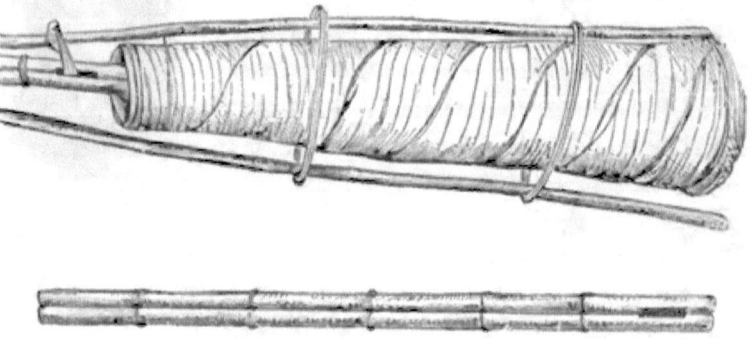

the arrow-root family. Round the tube are wrapped long strips of the tough bark of the Jébaru (*Parivoa grandiflora*). This covering descends in folds below the tube. The length of the instrument is from four to five feet. The illustration, which exhibits the *juruparis* with its cover and without it, has been taken from a specimen in the museum at Kew gardens. The mysteries connected with this trumpet are evidently founded on an old tradition from prehistoric Indian ancestors. *Jurupari* means "demon"; and with several Indian tribes on the Amazon customs and ceremonies still prevail in honour of Jurupari.

The Caroados, an Indian tribe in Brazil, have a war trumpet which closely resembles the *juruparis*. With this people it is the custom for the chief to give on his war trumpet the signal for battle, and to continue blowing as long as he wishes the battle to last. The trumpet is made of wood, and its sound is described by travellers as very deep but rather pleasant. The sound is easily produced, and its continuance does not require much exertion; but a peculiar vibration of the lips is necessary which requires practice. Another trumpet, the *turé*, is common with many Indian tribes on the Amazon who use it chiefly in war. It is made of a long and thick bamboo, and there is a split reed in the mouthpiece. It therefore partakes rather of the character of an oboe or clarinet. Its tone is described as loud and harsh. The *turé* is especially used by the sentinels of predatory hordes, who, mounted on a lofty tree, give the signal of attack to their comrades.

Again, the aborigines in Mexico had a curious contrivance of this kind, the *acocotl*, now more usually called *clarin*. The former word is its old Indian name, and the latter appears to have been first given to the instrument by the Spaniards. The *acocotl* consists of a very thin tube from eight to ten feet in length, and generally not quite straight but with some irregular curves. This tube, which is often not thicker than a couple of inches in diameter, terminates at one end in a sort of bell, and has at the other end a small mouthpiece resembling in shape that of a clarinet. The tube is made of the dry stalk of a plant which is common in Mexico, and which likewise the Indians call *acocotl*. The most singular characteristic of the instrument is that the performer does not blow into it, but inhales the air through it; or rather, he produces the sound by sucking the mouthpiece. It is said to require strong lungs to perform on the *acocotl* effectively according to Indian notions of taste.

The *botuto*, which Gumilla saw used by some tribes near the river Orinoco (of which we engrave two examples), was evidently

an ancient Indian contrivance, but appears to have fallen almost into oblivion during the last two centuries. It was made of baked clay and was commonly from three to four feet long: but some trumpets of this kind were of enormous size. The *botuto* with two bellies was usually made thicker than that with three bellies and emitted a deeper sound, which is described as having been really terrific. These trumpets were used on occasions of mourning and funeral dances. Alexander von Humboldt saw the *botuto* among some Indian tribes near the river Orinoco.

Besides those which have been noticed, other antique wind instruments of the Indians are mentioned by historians; but the descriptions given of them are too superficial to convey a

MUSICAL INSTRUMENTS.

distinct notion as to their form and purport. Several of these barbarous contrivances scarcely deserve to be classed with musical instruments. This may, for instance, be said of certain musical jars or earthen vessels producing sounds, which the Peruvians constructed for their amusement. These vessels were made double; and the sounds imitated the cries of animals or birds. A similar contrivance of the Indians in Chili, preserved in the museum at Santiago, is described by the traveller S. S. Hill as follows:—" It consists of two earthen vessels in the form of our india-rubber bottles, but somewhat larger, with a flat tube from four to six inches in length, uniting their necks near the top and slightly curved upwards, and with a small hole on the upper side one third of the length of the tube from one side of the necks. To produce the sounds the bottles were filled with water and suspended to the bough of a tree, or to a beam, by a string attached to the middle of the curved tube, and then swung backwards and forwards in such a manner as to cause each end to be alternately the highest and lowest, so that the water might pass backwards and forwards from one bottle to the other through the tube between them. By this means soothing sounds were produced which, it is said, were employed to lull to repose the drowsy chiefs who usually slept away the hottest hours of the day. In the meantime, as the bottles were porous, the water within them diminished by evaporation, and the sound died gradually away."

As regards instruments of percussion, a kind of drum deserves special notice on account of the ingenuity evinced in its construction. The Mexicans called it *teponaztli*. They generally made it of a single block of very hard wood, somewhat oblong square in shape, which they hollowed, leaving at each end a solid piece about three or four inches in thickness, and at its upper side a kind of sound-board about a quarter of an inch in thickness. In this sound-board, if it may be called so, they made three incisions; namely, two running parallel some distance lengthwise of the drum, and a third running across from one of these to the other just in the centre. By this means they obtained two vibrating tongues of wood which, when beaten with a stick, produced sounds as clearly defined as are those of our kettle drums. By

 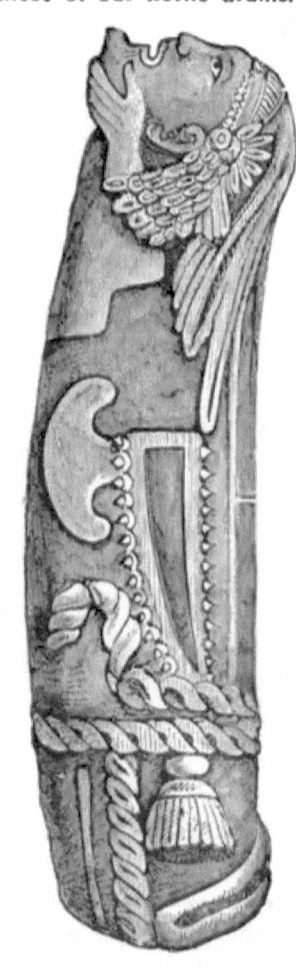

making one of the tongues thinner than the other they ensured two different sounds, the pitch of which they were enabled to regulate by shaving off more or less of the wood. The bottom of the drum they cut almost entirely open. The traveller, M. Nebel, was told by archæologists in Mexico that these instruments always contained the interval of a third, but on examining several specimens which he saw in museums he found some in which the two sounds stood towards each other in the relation of a fourth; while in others they constituted a fifth, in others a sixth, and in some even an octave. This is noteworthy in so far as it points to a conformity with our diatonic series of intervals, excepting the seventh.

The *teponaztli* (engraved above) was generally carved with various fanciful and ingenious designs. It was beaten with two drumsticks covered at the end with an elastic gum, called *ule*, which was obtained from the milky juice extracted from the ule-tree. Some of these drums were small enough to be carried on a string or strap suspended round the neck of the player; others, again, measured upwards of five feet in length, and their sound was so powerful that it could be heard at a distance of three miles. In some rare instances a specimen of the *teponaztli* is still preserved by the Indians in Mexico, especially among tribes who have been comparatively but little affected by intercourse with their European aggressors. Herr Heller saw such an instrument in the hands of the Indians of Huatusco—a village near Mirador in the Tierra templada, or temperate region, occupying the slopes of the Cordilleras. Its sound is described as so very loud as to be distinctly audible at an incredibly great distance. This circumstance, which has been noticed by several travellers, may per-

haps be owing in some measure to the condition of the atmosphere in Mexico.

Instruments of percussion constructed on a principle more or less similar to the *teponaztli* were in use in several other parts of America, as well as in Mexico.

Oviedo gives a drawing of a drum from San Domingo which, as

it shows distinctly both the upper and under side of the instrument, is here inserted.

The largest kind of Mexican *teponaztli* appears to have been generally of a cylindrical shape. Clavigero gives a drawing of such an instrument. Drums, also, constructed of skin or parchment in combination with wood were not unknown to the Indians. Of this description was, for instance, the *huehuetl* of the Aztecs in Mexico, which consisted, according to Clavigero, of a wooden cylinder somewhat above three feet in height, curiously carved and painted and covered at the top with carefully prepared deer-skin. And, what appears the most remarkable, the parchment (we are told) could be tightened or slackened by means of cords in nearly the same way as with our own drum. The *huehuetl* was not beaten with drumsticks but merely struck with the fingers, and much dexterity was required to strike it in the proper manner. Oviedo states that the Indians in Cuba had drums which were stretched with human skin. And Bernal Diaz relates that when he was with Cortés in Mexico they ascended together the *Teocalli* ("House of God"), a large temple in which human sacrifices were offered by the aborigines; and there the Spanish visitors saw a large drum which was made, Diaz tells us, with skins of great serpents. This "hellish instrument," as he calls it, produced, when struck, a doleful sound which was so loud that it could be heard at a distance of two leagues.

The name of the Peruvian drum was *huanca*: they had also an instrument of percussion, called *chhilchiles*, which appears to have been a sort of tambourine.

The rattle was likewise popular with the Indians before the discovery of America. The Mexicans called it *ajacaxtli*. In construction it was similar to the rattle at the present day commonly used by the Indians. It was oval or round in shape, and appears to have been usually made of a gourd into which holes were pierced, and to which a wooden handle was affixed. A number of little pebbles were enclosed in the hollowed gourd.

They were also made of pottery. . The little balls in the *ajacaxtli* of pottery, enclosed as they are, may at a first glance appear a puzzle. Probably, when the rattle was being formed they were attached to the inside as slightly as possible; and after the clay had been baked they were detached by means of an implement passed through the holes.

The Tezcucans (or Acolhuans) belonged to the same race as the Aztecs, whom they greatly surpassed in knowledge and social refinement. Nezahualcoyotl, a wise monarch of the Tezcucans, abhorred human sacrifices, and erected a large temple which he dedicated to "The unknown god, the cause of causes." This edifice had a tower nine stories high, on the top of which were placed a number of musical instruments of various kinds which were used to summon the worshippers to prayer. Respecting these instruments especial mention is made of a sonorous metal which was struck with a mallet. This is stated in a historical essay written by Ixtlilxochitl, a native of Mexico and of royal descent, who lived in the beginning of the seventeenth century, and who may be supposed to have been familiar with the musical practices of his countrymen. But whether the sonorous metal

alluded to was a gong or a bell is not clear from the vague record transmitted to us. That the bell was known to the Peruvians appears to be no longer doubtful, since a small copper specimen has been found in one of the old Peruvian tombs. This interesting relic is now deposited in the museum at Lima. M. de Castelnau has published a drawing of it, which is here reproduced. The Peruvians called their bells *chanrares:* but it remains questionable whether this name did not designate rather the so-called horse bells, which were certainly known to the Mexicans who called them *yotl*. It is noteworthy that these *yotl* are found figured in the picture-writings representing the various objects which the Aztecs used to pay as tribute to their sovereigns. The collection of Mexican antiquities in the British museum contains a cluster of yotl-bells. Being nearly round, they closely resemble the *Schellen* which the Germans are in the habit of affixing to their horses, particularly in the winter when they are driving their noiseless sledges.

Again, in south America sonorous stones are not unknown, and were used in olden time for musical purposes. The traveller G. T. Vigne saw among the Indian antiquities preserved in the town of Cuzco, in Peru, " a musical instrument of green sonorous stone, about a foot long, and an inch and a half wide, flat-sided, pointed at both ends, and arched at the back, where it was about a quarter of an inch thick, whence it diminished to an edge, like the blade of a knife . . . . . In the middle of the back was a small hole, through which a piece of string was passed; and when suspended and struck by any hard substance a singularly musical note was produced." Humboldt mentions the Amazon-stone, which on being struck by a hard substance yields a metallic sound. It was formerly cut by the American Indians into very thin plates, perforated in the centre and suspended by a string. These plates were remarkably sonorous. This kind of stone is not, as might be conjectured from its name, found exclusively near the Amazon. The name was given to it as well as to the river by the first European visitors to America, in allusion to the female warriors respecting whom strange stories are told. The natives pretending, according to an ancient tradition, that the stone came from the country of "Women without husbands," or "Women living alone."

As regards the ancient stringed instruments of the American Indians our information is indeed but scanty. Clavigero says that the Mexicans were entirely unacquainted with stringed instruments: a statement the correctness of which is questionable, considering the stage of civilization to which these people had attained. At any rate, we generally find one or other kind of such instruments with nations whose intellectual progress and social condition are decidedly inferior. The Aztecs had many claims to the character of a civilized community and (as before said) the Tezcucans were even more advanced in the cultivation of the arts and sciences than the Aztecs. "The best histories," Prescott observes, "the best poems, the best code of laws, the purest dialect, were all allowed to be Tezcucan. The Aztecs rivalled their neighbours in splendour of living, and even in the magnificence of their structures. They displayed a pomp and ostentatious pageantry, truly Asiatic." Unfortunately historians are sometimes not sufficiently discerning in their communications respecting musical questions. J. Ranking, in describing the grandeur of the establishment maintained by Montezuma, says that during the repasts of this monarch "there was music of fiddle, flute, snail-shell, a kettle-drum, and other strange instruments." But as this writer does not indicate the source whence he drew his information respecting Montezuma's orchestra including the fiddle, the assertion deserves scarcely a passing notice.

The Peruvians possessed a stringed instrument, called *tinya*, which was provided with five or seven strings. To conjecture from the unsatisfactory account of it transmitted to us, the *tinya* appears to have been a kind of guitar. Considering the fragility of the materials of which such instruments are generally constructed, it is perhaps not surprising that we do not meet with any specimens of them in the museums of American antiquities.

A few remarks will not be out of place here referring to the musical performances of the ancient Indians; since an acquaintance with the nature of the performances is likely to afford additional assistance in appreciating the characteristics of the instruments. In Peru, where the military system was carefully organised, each division of the army had its trumpeters, called *cqueppacamayo*, and its drummers, called *huancarcamayo*. When the Inca returned with his troops victorious from battle his first act was to repair to the temple of the Sun in order to offer up thanksgiving; and after the conclusion of this ceremony the people celebrated the event with festivities, of which music and dancing constituted a principal part. Musical performances appear to have been considered indispensable on occasions of public celebrations; and frequent mention is made of them by historians who have described the festivals annually observed by the Peruvians.

About the month of October the Peruvians celebrated a solemn feast in honour of the dead, at which ceremony they executed lugubrious songs and plaintive instrumental music. Compositions of a similar character were performed on occasion of the decease of a monarch. As soon as it was made known to the people that their Inca had been "called home to the mansions of his father the sun" they prepared to celebrate his obsequies with becoming solemnity. Prescott, in his graphic description of these observances, says: "At stated intervals, for a year, the people assembled to renew the expressions of their sorrow; processions were made displaying the banner of the departed monarch; bards and minstrels were appointed to chronicle his achievements, and their songs continued to be rehearsed at high festivals in the presence of the reigning monarch,—thus stimulating the living by the glorious example of the dead." The Peruvians had also particular agricultural songs, which they were in the habit of singing while engaged in tilling the lands of the Inca; a duty which devolved upon the whole nation. The subject of these songs, or rather hymns, referred especially to the noble deeds and glorious achievements of the Inca and his dynasty. While thus singing, the labourers regulated their work to the rhythm of the music, thereby ensuring a pleasant excitement and a stimulant in their occupation, like soldiers regulating their steps to the music of the military band. These hymns pleased the Spanish invaders so greatly that they not only adopted several of them but also composed some in a similar form and style. This appears, however, to have been the case rather with the poetry than with the music.

The name of the Peruvian elegiac songs was *haravi*. Some tunes of these songs, pronounced to be genuine specimens, have been published in recent works; but their genuineness is questionable. At all events they must have been much tampered with, as they exhibit exactly the form of the Spanish *bolero*. Even allowing that the melodies of these compositions have been derived from Peruvian *harivaris*, it is impossible to determine with any degree of certainty how much in them has been retained of the original tunes, and how much has been supplied besides the harmony, which is entirely an addition of the European arranger. The Peruvians had minstrels, called *haravecs* (*i.e.*, "inventors"), whose occupation it was to compose and to recite the *haravis*.

The Mexicans possessed a class of songs which served as a record of historical events. Furthermore they had war-songs, love-songs, and other secular vocal compositions, as well as sacred chants, in the practice of which boys were instructed by the priests in order that they might assist in the musical performances of the temple. It appertained to the office of the priests to burn incense, and to perform music in the temple at stated times of the day. The commencement of the religious observances which took place regularly at sunrise, at mid-day, at sunset, and at midnight, was announced by signals blown on trumpets and pipes. Persons of high position retained in their service professional musicians whose duty it was to compose ballads, and to perform vocal music with instrumental accompaniment. The nobles themselves, and occasionally even the monarch, not unfrequently delighted in composing ballads and odes.

Especially to be noticed is the institution termed "Council of music," which the wise monarch Nezahualcoyotl founded in Tezcuco. This institution was not intended exclusively for promoting the cultivation of music; its aim comprised the advancement of various arts, and of sciences such as history, astronomy, &c. In fact, it was an academy for general education. Probably no better evidence could be cited testifying to the remarkable intellectual attainments of the Mexican Indians before the discovery of America than this council of music. Although in some respects it appears to have resembled the board of music of the Chinese, it was planned on a more enlightened and more comprehensive principle. The Chinese "board of music," called *Yo Poo*, is an office connected with the *Lê Poo* or "board of rites," established by the imperial government at Peking. The principal object of the board of rites is to regulate the ceremonies on occasions of sacrifices offered to the gods; of festivals and certain court solemnities; of military reviews; of presentations, congratulations, marriages, deaths, burials,—in short, concerning almost every possible event in social and public life.

The reader is probably aware that in one of the various hypotheses which have been advanced respecting the Asiatic origin of the American Indians China is assigned to them as their ancient home. Some historians suppose them to be emigrants from Mongolia, Thibet, or Hindustan; others maintain that they are the offspring of Phœnician colonists who settled in central America. Even more curious are the arguments of certain inquirers who have no doubt whatever that the ancestors of the American Indians were the lost ten tribes of Israel, of whom since about the time of the Babylonian captivity history is silent. Whatever may be thought as to which particular one of these speculations hits the truth, they certainly have all proved useful in so far as they have made ethnologists more exactly acquainted with the habits and predilections of the American aborigines than would otherwise have been the case. For, as the advocates of each hypothesis have carefully collected and adduced every evidence they were able to obtain tending to support their views, the result is that (so to say) no stone has been left unturned. Nevertheless, any such hints as suggest themselves from an examination of musical instruments have hitherto remained unheeded. It may therefore perhaps interest the reader to have his attention drawn to a few suggestive similarities occurring between instruments of the American Indians and of certain nations inhabiting the eastern hemisphere.

We have seen that the Mexican pipe and the Peruvian syrinx were purposely constructed so as to produce the intervals of the pentatonic scale only. There are some additional indications of this scale having been at one time in use with the American Indians. For instance, the music of the Peruvian dance *cachua* is described as having been very similar to some Scotch national dances; and the most conspicuous characteristics of the Scotch tunes are occasioned by the frequently exclusive employment of intervals appertaining to the pentatonic scale. We find precisely the same series of intervals adopted on certain Chinese instruments, and evidences are not wanting of the pentatonic scale having been popular among various races in Asia at a remote period. The series of intervals appertaining to the Chiriqui pipe, mentioned page 61, consisted of a semitone and two whole tones, like the *tetrachord* of the ancient Greeks.

In the Peruvian *huayra-puhura* made of talc some of the pipes possess lateral holes. This contrivance, which is rather unusual, occurs on the Chinese *cheng*. The *chayna*, mentioned page 64, seems to have been provided with a reed, like the oboe: and in Hindustan we find a species of oboe called *shehna*. The *turé* of the Indian tribes on the Amazon, mentioned page 69, reminds us of the trumpets *tooree*, or *tootooree*, of the Hindus. The name appears to have been known also to the Arabs; but there is no indication whatever of its having been transmitted to the peninsula by the Moors, and afterwards to south America by the Portuguese and Spaniards.

The wooden tongues in the drum *teponaztli* may be considered as a contrivance exclusively of the ancient American Indians. Nevertheless a construction nearly akin to it may be observed in certain drums of the Tonga and Feejee islanders, and of the natives of some islands in Torres strait. Likewise some negro tribes in western and central Africa have certain instruments of percussion which are constructed on a principle somewhat reminding us of the *teponaztli*. The method of bracing the drum by means of cords, as exhibited in the *huchueil* of the Mexican Indians, is evidently of very high antiquity in the east. It was known to the ancient Egyptians.

Rattles, pandean pipes made of reed, and conch trumpets, are found almost all over the world, wherever the materials of which they are constructed are easily obtainable. Still, it may be noteworthy that the Mexicans employed the conch trumpet in their religious observances apparently in much the same way as it is used in the Buddhist worship of the Thibetans and Kalmuks.

As regards the sonorous metal in the great temple at Tezcuco some inquirers are sure that it was a gong: but it must be borne in mind that these inquirers detect everywhere traces proving an invasion of the Mongols, which they maintain to have happened about six hundred years ago. Had they been acquainted with the little Peruvian bell (engraved on page 75) they would have had more tangible musical evidence in support of their theory than the supposed gong; for this bell certainly bears a suggestive resemblance to the little hand-bell which the Buddhists use in their religious ceremonies.

The Peruvians interpolated certain songs, especially those which they were in the habit of singing while cultivating the fields, with the word *hailli* which signified "Triumph." As the subject of these compositions was principally the glorification of the Inca, the burden *hailli* is perhaps all the more likely to remind Europeans of the Hebrew *hallelujah*. Moreover, Adair, who lived among the Indians of north America during a period of about forty years, speaks of some other words which he found used as burdens in hymns sung on solemn occasions, and which appeared to him to correspond with certain Hebrew words of a sacred import.

As regards the musical accomplishments of the Indian tribes at the present day they are far below the standard which we have found among their ancestors. A period of three hundred years of oppression has evidently had the effect of subduing the melodious expressions of happiness and contentedness which in former times appear to have been quite as prevalent with the Indians as they generally are with independent and flourishing nations. The innate talent for music evinced by those of the North American Indians who were converted to Christianity soon after the emigration of the puritans to New England is very favourably commented on by some old writers. In the year 1661 John Elliot published a translation of the psalms into Indian verse. The singing of these metrical psalms by the Indian converts in their places of worship appears to have been actually superior to the sacred vocal performances of their Christian brethren from Europe; for we find it described by several witnesses as "excellent" and "most ravishing."

In other parts of America the catholic priests from Spain did not neglect to turn to account the susceptibility of the Indians for music. Thus, in central America the Dominicans composed as early as in the middle of the sixteenth century a sacred poem in the Guatemalian dialect containing a narrative of the most important events recorded in the Bible. This production they sang to the natives, and to enhance the effect they accompanied the singing with musical instruments. The alluring music soon captivated the heart of a powerful cazique, who was thus induced to adopt the doctrines embodied in the composition, and to diffuse them among his subjects who likewise delighted in the performances. In Peru a similar experiment, resorted to by the priests who accompanied Pizarro's expedition, proved equally successful. They dramatized certain scenes in the life of Christ and represented them with music, which so greatly fascinated the Indians that many of them readily embraced the new faith. Nor are these entertainments dispensed with even at the present day by the Indian Christians, especially in the village churches of the Sierra in Peru; and as several religious ceremonies have been retained by these people from their heathen forefathers, it may be conjectured that their sacred musical performances also retain much of their ancient heathen character.

Most of the musical instruments found among the American Indians at the present day are evidently genuine old Indian contrivances as they existed long before the discovery of America. Take, for example, the peculiarly shaped rattles, drums, flutes, and whistles of the North American Indians, of which some specimens in the Kensington museum are described in the large catalogue. A few African instruments, introduced by the negro slaves, are now occasionally found in the hands of the Indians, and have been by some travellers erroneously described as genuine Indian inventions. This is the case with the African *marimba*, which has become rather popular with the natives of Guatemala in central America: but such adaptations are very easily discernible.

CHAPTER VII.

EUROPEAN NATIONS DURING THE MIDDLE AGES.

MANY representations of musical instruments of the middle ages have been preserved in manuscripts, as well as in sculptures and paintings forming ornamental portions of churches and other buildings. Valuable facts and hints are obtainable from these evidences, provided they are judiciously selected and carefully examined. The subject is, however, so large that only a few observations on the most interesting instruments can be offered here. Unfortunately there still prevails much uncertainty respecting several of the earliest representations as to the precise century from which they date, and there is reason to believe that in some instances the archæological zeal of musical investigators has assigned a higher antiquity to such discoveries than can be satisfactorily proved.

It appears certain that the most ancient European instruments known to us were in form and construction more like the Asiatic than was the case with later ones. Before a nation has attained to a rather high degree of civilisation its progress in the cultivation of music, as an art, is very slow indeed. The instruments found at the present day in Asia are scarcely superior to those which were in use among oriental nations about three thousand years ago. It is, therefore, perhaps not surprising that no material improvement is perceptible in the construction of the instruments of European countries during the lapse of nearly a thousand years. True, evidences to be relied on referring to the first five or six centuries of the Christian era are but scanty; although indications are not wanting which may help the reflecting musician.

There are some early monuments of Christian art dating from the fourth century in which the lyre is represented. In one of them Christ is depicted as Apollo touching the lyre. This instrument occurs at an early period in western Europe as used in popular pastimes. In an Anglo-saxon manuscript of the ninth century in the British museum (Cleopatra C. VIII.) are the figures of two gleemen, one playing the lyre and the other a double-pipe. M. de Coussemaker has published in the "Annales Archéologiques" the figure of a crowned personage playing the lyre, which he found in a manuscript of the ninth or tenth century in the library at Angers. The player twangs the strings with his fingers, while the Anglo-saxon gleeman before mentioned uses a plectrum.

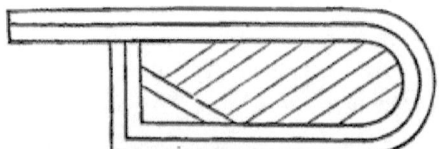

Cithara was a name applied to several stringed instruments greatly varying in form, power of sound, and compass. The illustration represents a cithara from a manuscript of the ninth century, formerly in the library of the great monastery of St. Blasius in the Black Forest. When in the year 1768 the monastery was destroyed by fire, this valuable book perished in the flames; fortunately the celebrated abbot Gerbert possessed tracings of the illustrations, which were saved from destruction. He published them, in the year 1774, in his work "De cantu et musica sacra." Several

illustrations in the following pages, it will be seen, have been derived from this interesting source. As the older works on music were generally written in Latin we do not learn

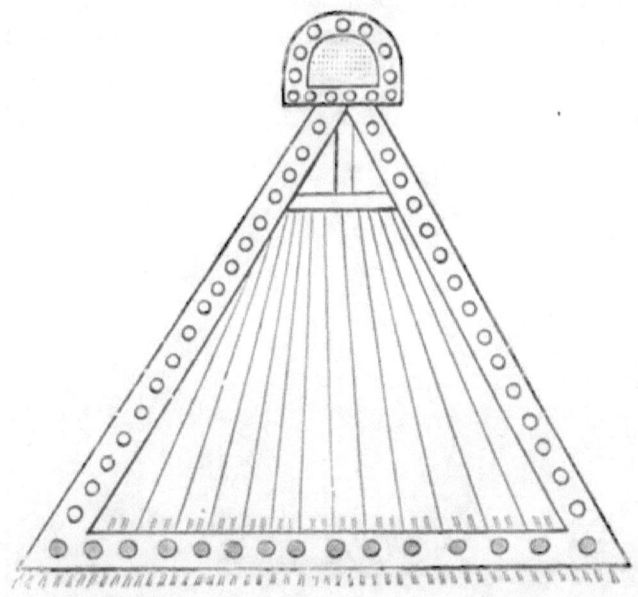

from them the popular names of the instruments; the writers merely adopted such Latin names as they thought the most appropriate. Thus, for instance, a very simple stringed instrument of a triangular shape, and a somewhat similar one of a square shape were designated by the name of *psalterium*; and we further give a woodcut of the square

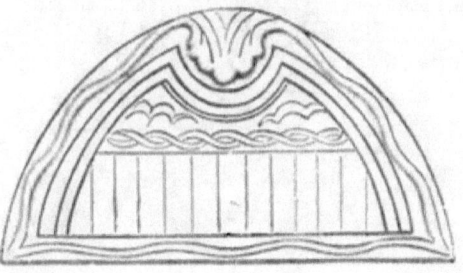

kind (p. 86), and of a *cithara* (above) from the same manuscript.

This last instrument is evidently an improvement upon the

triangular psalterium, because it has a sort of small sound-board at the top. Scarcely better, with regard to acoustics, appears to have been the instrument designated as *nablum*, which we engrave (p. 87) from a manuscript of the ninth century at Angers.

A small psalterium with strings placed over a sound-board was

apparently the prototype of the *citole;* a kind of dulcimer which was played with the fingers. The names were not only often vaguely applied by the mediæval writers but they changed also in almost every century. The psalterium, or psalterion (Italian *salterio*, English *psaltery*), of the fourteenth century and later had the trapezium shape of the dulcimer.

The Anglo-saxons frequently accompanied their vocal effusions with a harp, more or less triangular in shape,—an instrument which may be considered rather as constituting the transition of the lyre into the harp. The representation of king David playing the harp is from an Anglo-saxon manuscript of the beginning of the eleventh century, in the British museum. The harp was especially popular in central and northern Europe, and was the favourite instrument of the German and Celtic bards and of the Scandinavian skalds. In the next illustration from the manuscript of the monastery of St. Blasius twelve strings and two sound holes are given to it. A harp similar in form and size, but without the front pillar, was known to the ancient Egyptians. Perhaps the addition was also non-existant in the earliest specimens appertaining to European nations; and a sculptured figure of a small harp constructed like the ancient eastern harp has been discovered in the old church of Ullard in the county of Kilkenny. Of this curious relic, which is said to date from a period anterior to the year 800, a fac-simile taken from Bunting's "Ancient Music of Ireland" is given (p. 91). As Bunting

was the first who drew attention to this sculpture his account of it may interest the reader. "The drawing" he says "is taken from one of the ornamental compartments of a sculptured cross, at the old church of Ullard. From the style of the workmanship, as well as from the worn condition of the cross, it seems older than the similar

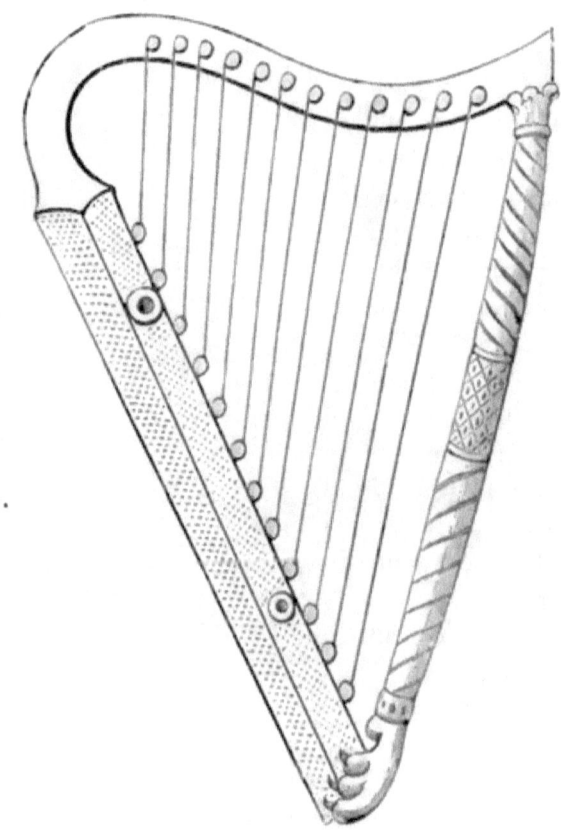

monument at Monasterboice which is known to have been set up before the year 830. The sculpture is rude; the circular rim which binds the arms of the cross together is not pierced in the quadrants, and many of the figures originally in relievo are now wholly abraded. It is difficult to determine whether the number of strings represented is six or seven; but, as has been already remarked, accuracy in this respect cannot be expected either in

sculptures or in many picturesque drawings." The Finns had a harp (*harpu, kantele*) with a similar frame, devoid of a front pillar, still in use until the commencement of the present century.

One of the most interesting stringed instruments of the middle ages is the *rotta* (German, *rotte;* English, *rote*). It was sounded by twanging the strings, and also by the application of the bow. The first method was, of course, the elder one. There can hardly be a doubt that when the bow came into use it was applied to certain popular instruments which previously had been treated like the *cithara* or the *psalterium*. The

Hindus at the present day use their *suroda* sometimes as a

lute and sometimes as a fiddle. In some measure we do the same with the violin by playing occasionally *pizzicato*. The *rotta* (shown p. 91) from the manuscript of St. Blasius is called in Gerbert's work *cithara teutonica*, while the harp is called

cithara anglica; from which it would appear that the former was regarded as preeminently a German instrument. Possibly its name may have been originally *chrotta* and the continental nations may have adopted it from the Celtic races of the British isles, dropping the guttural sound. This hypothesis is, however, one of ose which have been advanced by some musical historians without any satisfactory evidence.

We engrave also another representation of David playing on the *rotta*, from a psalter of the seventh century in the British museum (Cott. Vesp. A. I). According to tradition, this psalter is one of the manuscripts which were sent by pope Gregory to St. Augustine. The instrument much resembles the lyre in the hand of the musician (see p. 22) who is supposed to be a Hebrew of the time of Joseph. In the *rotta* the ancient Asiatic lyre is easily to be recognized. An illumination of king David playing the *rotta* forms the frontispiece of a manuscript of the eighth century preserved in the cathedral library of Durham; and which is musically interesting inasmuch as it represents a *rotta* of an oblong square shape like that just noticed and resembling the Welsh *crwth*. It has only five strings which the performer twangs with his fingers. Again, a very interesting representation (which we engrave) of the Psalmist with a kind of *rotta* occurs in a manu-

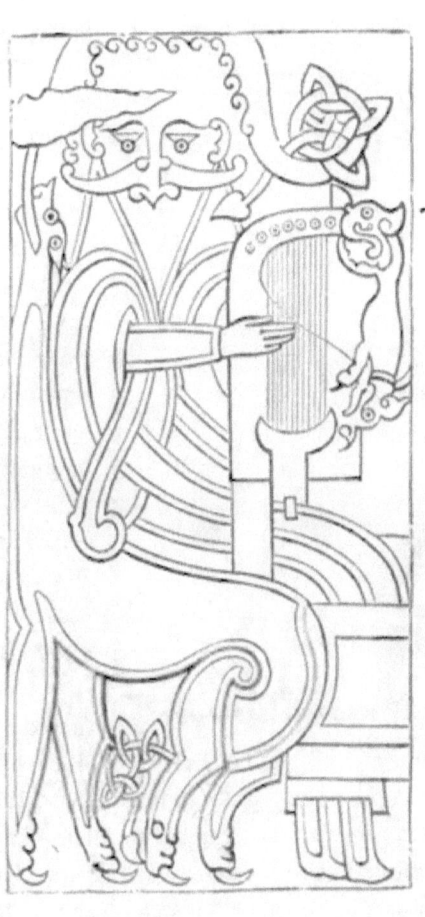

script of the tenth century, in the British museum (Vitellius F. XI.). The manuscript has been much injured by a fire in the year 1731; but professor Westwood has succeeded, with great care, and with the aid of a magnifying glass, in making out the lines of the figure. As it has been ascertained that the psalter is written in the Irish semi-uncial character it is highly probable that the kind of *rotta* represents the Irish *cionar cruit*, which was played by twanging the strings and also by the application of a bow. Unfortunately we possess no well-authenticated representation of the Welsh *crwth* of an early period; otherwise we should in all probability find it played with the fingers, or with a plectrum. Venantius Fortunatus, an Italian who lived in the second half of the sixth century, mentions in a poem the "Chrotta Britanna." He does not, however, allude to the bow, and there is no reason to suppose that it existed in England. Howbeit, the Welsh *crwth* (Anglo-saxon, *crudh ;* English, *crowd*) is only known as a species of fiddle closely resembling the *rotta*, but having a fingerboard in the middle of the open frame and being strung with only a few strings; while the *rotta* had sometimes above twenty strings. As it may interest the reader to examine

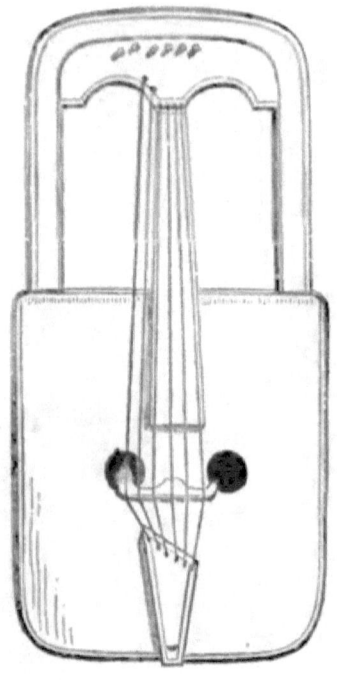

the form of the modern *crwth* we give a woodcut of it. Edward Jones, in his "Musical and poetical relicks of the Welsh bards," records that the Welsh had before this kind of *crwth* a three-stringed one called "Crwth Trithant," which was, he says, "a sort of violin, or more properly a rebeck." The three-stringed *crwth* was chiefly used by the inferior class of bards; and was probably the Moorish fiddle which is still the favourite instrument of the itinerant bards of the Bretons in France, who call it *rébek*. The Bretons, it will be remembered, are close kinsmen of the Welsh.

A player on the *crwth* or *crowd* (a crowder) from a bas-relief on the under part of the seats of the choir in Worcester cathedral (engraved p. 95) dates from the twelfth or thirteenth century; and we give (p. 96) a copy of an illumination from a manuscript in the Bibliothèque royale at Paris of the eleventh century. The player wears a crown on his head; and in the original some musicians placed at his side are performing on the psalterium and other instruments. These last are figured with uncovered heads; whence M. de Coussemaker concludes that the *crout* was considered by the artist who drew the figures as the noblest instrument. It was probably identical with the *rotta* of the same century on the continent.

An interesting drawing of an Anglo-saxon fiddle—or *fithele*, as it was called—is given in a manuscript of the eleventh century in the British museum (Cotton, Tiberius, c. 6). The instrument is of a pear shape, with four strings, and the bridge is not indicated. A German fiddle of the ninth century, called *lyra*, copied by Gerbert from the manuscript of St. Blasius, has only one string. These are shown in the woodcuts (p. 97). Other records of the employment of the fiddle-bow in Germany in

the twelfth and thirteenth centuries are not wanting. For instance, in the famous 'Nibelungenlied' Volker is described as wielding the fiddle bow not less dexterously than the sword. And in 'Chronicon picturatum Brunswicense' of the year 1203, the following miraculous sign is recorded as having occurred in the village of Ossemer: "On Wednesday in Whitsun-week, while the parson was fiddling to his peasants who were dancing, there came a flash of lightning and struck the parson's arm which held the fiddle-bow, and killed twenty-four people on the spot."

Among the oldest representations of performers on instruments of the violin kind found in England those deserve to be noticed which are painted on the interior of the roof of Peterborough cathedral. They are said to date from the twelfth century. One of these figures is particularly interesting on account of the surprising resemblance which his instrument bears to our present violin. Not only the incurvations on the sides of the body but also the two sound-holes are nearly identical in shape with those made at the present day. Respecting the reliance to be placed on such evidence, it is necessary to state that the roof, originally constructed between the years 1177 and 1194, was thoroughly repaired in the year 1835. Although we find it asserted that "the greatest care was taken to retain every part, or to restore it to its original state, so that the figures, even where retouched, are in effect the same as when first painted," it nevertheless remains a debatable question whether the restorers have not admitted some slight alterations, and have thereby somewhat modernised the appearance of the instruments. A slight touch with the brush at the sound-holes, the screws, or the curvatures, would suffice to produce modifications which might to the artist appear as being only a renovation of the original representation, but which to the musical investigator greatly impair the value of the

evidence. Sculptures are, therefore, more to be relied upon in evidence than frescoes.

CHAPTER VIII.

The construction of the *organistrum* requires but little explanation. A glance at the finger-board reveals at once that the different tones were obtained by raising the keys placed on the neck under the strings, and that the keys were raised by means of the handles at the side of the neck. Of the two bridges shown on the body, the one situated nearest the middle was formed by a wheel in the inside, which projected through the sound-board. The wheel which slightly touched the strings vibrated them by friction when turned by the handle at the end. The order of intervals was *c, d, e, f, g, a, b-flat, b-natural, c,* and were obtainable on the highest string. There is reason to suppose that the other two strings were generally tuned a fifth and an octave below the highest. The *organistrum* may be regarded as the predecessor of the hurdy-gurdy, and was a rather cumbrous contrivance. Two persons seem to have been required to sound it, one to turn the handle and the other to manage the keys. Thus it is generally represented in mediæval concerts.

The *monochord* (p. 100) was mounted with a single string stretched over two bridges which were fixed on an oblong box. The string could be tightened or slackened by means of a turning screw inserted into one end of the box. The intervals of the scale were marked on the side, and were regulated by a sort of movable bridge placed beneath the string when required. As might be expected, the

monochord was chiefly used by theorists; for any musical performance it was but little suitable. About a thousand years ago when this monochord was in use the musical scale was diatonic, with the exception of the interval of the seventh, which was chromatic inasmuch as both *b-flat* and *b-natural* formed part of the scale. The notation on the preceding page exhibits the compass as well as the order of intervals adhered to about the tenth century.

This ought to be borne in mind in examining the representations of musical instruments transmitted to us from that period.

As regards the wind instruments popular during the middle ages, some were of quaint form as well as of rude construction.

The *chorus*, or *choron*, had either one or two tubes, as in the woodcut page 101. There were several varieties of this instrument; sometimes it was constructed with a bladder into which the tube is inserted; this kind of *chorus* resembled the bagpipe; another kind resembled the *poongi* of the Hindus, mentioned page 51. The name *chorus* was also applied to certain stringed instruments. One of these had much the form of the *cithara*, page 86. It appears however, probable that *chorus* or

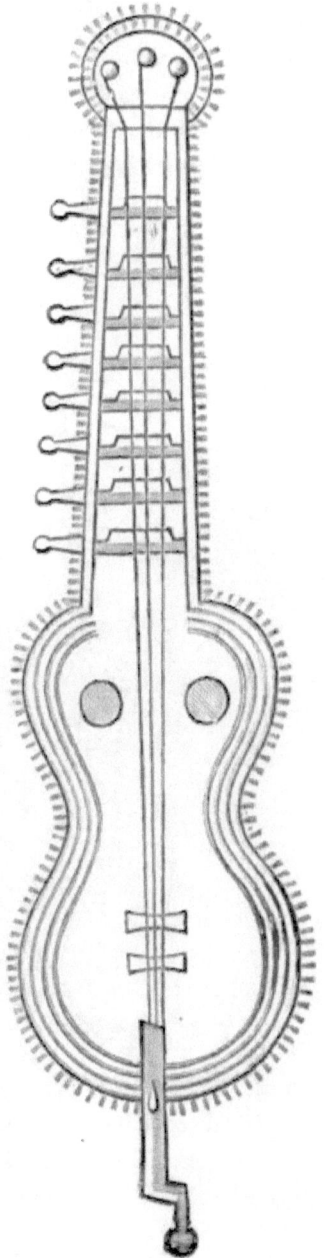

choron originally designated a horn (Hebrew, *Keren;* Greek, *Keras;* Latin, *cornu*).

The flutes of the middle ages were blown at the end, like the flageolet. Of the *syrinx* there are extant some illustrations of the ninth and tenth centuries, which exhibit the instrument with a

number of tubes tied together, just like the Pandean pipe still in use. In one specimen engraved (page 102) from a manuscript of the eleventh century the tubes were inserted into a bowl-shaped box. This is probably the *frestele*, *fretel*, or *fretiau*, which in the twelfth and thirteenth centuries was in favour with the French ménétriers.

Some large Anglo-saxon trumpets may be seen in a manuscript of the eighth century in the British museum. The largest kind of trumpet was placed on a stand when blown. Of the *oliphant*, or hunting horn, some fine specimens are in the South Kensington

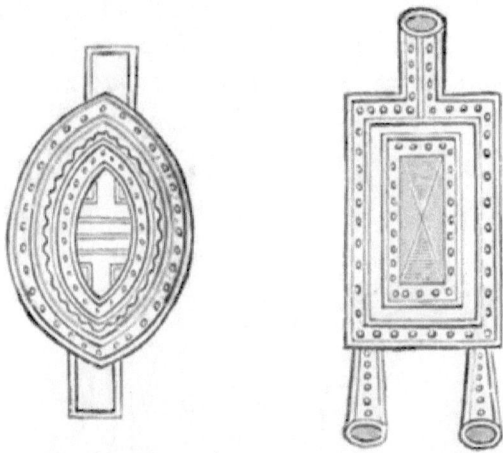

collection. The *sackbut* (of which we give a woodcut) probably

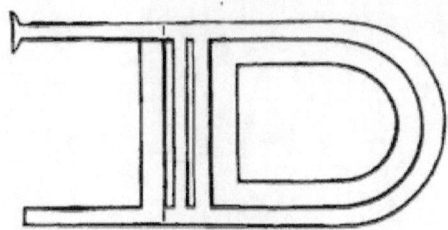

made of metal, could be drawn out to alter the pitch of sound. The sackbut of the ninth century had, however, a very different shape to that in use about three centuries ago, and much more resembled the present *trombone*. The name *sackbut* is supposed to be a corruption of *sambuca*. The French, about the fifteenth century, called it *sacqueboute* and *saquebutte*.

The most important wind instrument—in fact, the king of all the musical instruments—is the organ.

The *pneumatic organ* is sculptured on an obelisk which was erected in Constantinople under Theodosius the great, towards the end of the fourth century. The bellows were pressed by men standing on them: see page 103. This interesting monument also exhibits performers on the double flute. The *hydraulic organ*, which **is recorded** to have been already known about two hundred years before the Christian **era, was according** to some statements occasionally employed in churches during the earlier centuries of the middle ages. Probably it was more frequently heard in secular entertainments for which it was more suitable; and at the begin-

ning of the fourteenth century appears to have been entirely supplanted by the pneumatic organ. The earliest organs had only about a dozen pipes. The largest, which were made about nine hundred years ago, had only three octaves, in which the chromatic intervals did not occur. Some progress in the construction of the organ is exhibited in an illustration (engraved p. 104) dating from the twelfth century, in a psalter of Eadwine, in the library of Trinity college, Cambridge. The instrument has ten pipes, or perhaps fourteen, as four of them appear to be double pipes. It required four men exerting all their power to produce the necessary wind, and two men to play the instrument. Moreover, both players seem also to be busily engaged in directing the blowers about the proper supply of wind. Six men and only fourteen pipes! It must be admitted that since the twelfth century some progress has been made, at all events, in the construction of the organ.

The pedal is generally believed to have been invented by Bernhard, a German, who lived in Venice about the year 1470. There are, however, indications extant pointing to an earlier date of its invention. Perhaps Bernhard was the first who, by adopting a more practicable construction, made the pedal more generally known. On the earliest organs the keys of the finger-board were of enormous size, compared with those of the present day; so that a finger-board with only nine keys had a breadth of from four to five feet. The organist struck the keys down with his fist, as is done in playing the *carillon* still in use on the continent, of which presently some account will be given.

Of the little portable organ, known as the *regal* or *regals*, often tastefully shaped and embellished, some interesting sculptured representations are still extant in the old ecclesiastical edifices of

England and Scotland. There is, for instance, in Beverley minster a figure of a man playing on a single regal, or a regal provided with only one set of pipes; and in Melrose abbey the figure of an angel holding in his arms a double regal, the pipes of which are in two sets. The regal generally had keys like those of the organ but smaller. A painting in the national Gallery, by Melozzo da Forli who lived in the fifteenth century, contains a regal which has keys of a peculiar shape, rather resembling the pistons of certain brass instruments. The illustration has been drawn from that painting.

To avoid misapprehension, it is necessary to mention that the name *regal* (or *regals*, *rigols*) was also applied to an instrument of percussion with sonorous slabs of wood. This contrivance was, in short, a kind of harmonica, resembling in shape as well as in the principle of its construction the little glass harmonica, a mere toy, in which slips of glass are arranged according to our musical scale. In England it appears to have been still known in the beginning of the eighteenth century. Grassineau describes the "Rigols" as "a kind of musical instrument consisting of several sticks bound together, only separated by beads. It makes a tolerable harmony, being well struck with a ball at the end of a stick." In the earlier centuries of the middle ages there appear to have been some instruments of percussion in favour, to which Grassineau's expression "a tolerable harmony" would scarcely have been applicable. Drums, of course, were known; and their rhythmical noise must have been soft music, compared with the shrill sounds of the *cymbalum;*

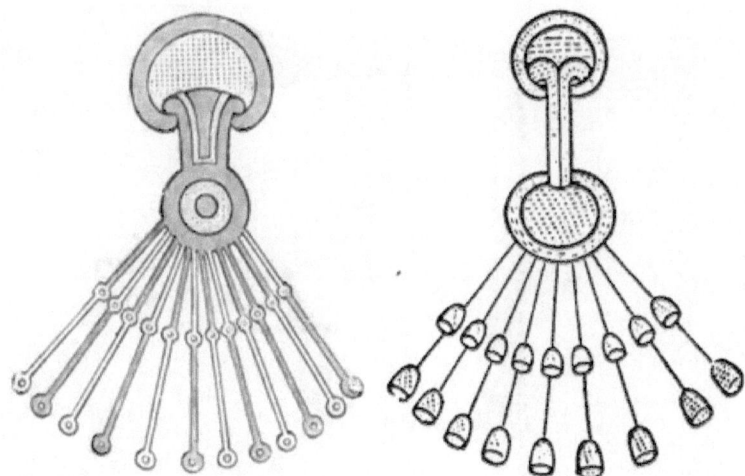

a contrivance consisting of a number of metal plates suspended on cords, so that they could be clashed together simultaneously; or with the clangour of the *cymbalum* constructed with bells instead of plates; or with the piercing noise of the *bunibulum*, or *bombulom;* an instrument which consisted of an angular frame to which were loosely attached metal plates of various shapes and sizes. The lower part of the frame constituted the handle : and to produce the noise it evidently was shaken somewhat like the sistrum of the ancient Egyptians. We give woodcuts of the three instruments.

The *triangle* nearly resembled the instrument of this name in use at the present day; it was more elegant in shape and had some metal ornamentation in the middle.

The *tintinnabulum* consisted of a number of bells arranged in regular order and suspended in a frame.

CHAPTER IX.

RESPECTING the orchestras, or musical bands, represented on monuments of the middle ages, there can hardly be a doubt that the artists who sculptured them were not unfrequently led by their imagination rather than by an adherence to actual fact. It is, however, not likely that they introduced into such representations instruments that were never admitted in the orchestras, and which would have appeared inappropriate to the contemporaries of the artists. An examination of one or two of the orchestras may therefore find a place here, especially as they throw some additional light upon the characteristics of the instrumental music of mediæval time.

A very interesting group of music performers dating, it is said, from the end of the eleventh century is preserved in a bas-relief which formerly ornamented the abbey of St. Georges de Boscherville and which is now removed to the museum of Rouen. The orchestra comprises twelve performers, most of whom wear a crown. The first of them plays upon a viol, which he holds between his knees as the violoncello is held. His instrument is scarcely as large as the smallest viola da gamba. By his side are a royal lady and her attendant, the former playing on an *organistrum* of which the latter is turning the wheel. Next to these is represented a performer on a *syrinx* of the kind shown in the engraving p. 112; and next to him a performer on a stringed instrument resembling a lute, which, however, is too much dilapidated to be recognisable. Then we have a musician with a small stringed instrument resembling the *nablum*, p. 87. The next musician, also represented as a royal

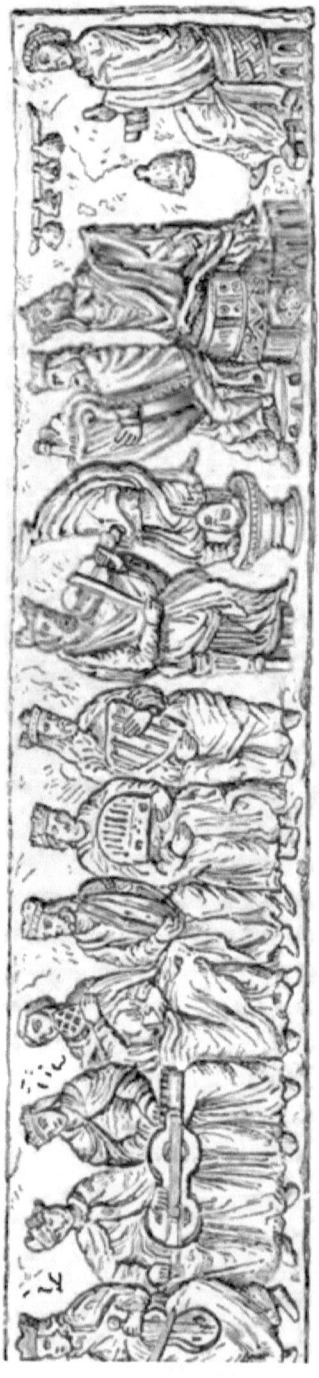

personage, plays on a small species of harp. Then follows a crowned musician playing the viol which he holds in almost precisely the same manner as the violin is held. Again, another, likewise crowned, plays upon a harp, using with the right hand a plectrum and with the left hand merely his fingers. The last two performers, apparently a gentleman and a gentlewoman, are engaged in striking the *tintinnabulum*,—a set of bells in a frame.

In this group of crowned minstrels the sculptor has introduced a tumbler standing on his head, perhaps the vocalist of the company, as he has no instrument to play upon. Possibly the sculptor desired to symbolise the hilarious effects which music is capable of producing, as well as its elevating influence upon the devotional feelings.

The two positions in which we find the viol held is worthy of notice, inasmuch as it refers the inquirer further back than might be expected for the origin of our peculiar method of holding the violin, and the violoncello, in playing. There were several kinds of the viol in use differing in size and in compass of sound. The most common number of strings was five, and it was tuned in various ways. One kind had a string

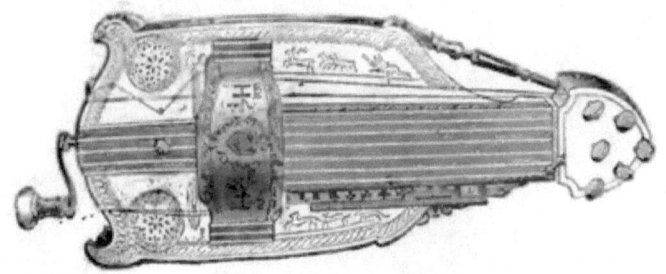

tuned to the note  running at the side of the finger-board instead of over it; this string was, therefore, only capable of producing a single tone. The four other strings were tuned thus:  Two other species, on which all the strings were placed over the finger-board, were tuned:  and:  The woodcut above represents a very beautiful *vielle;* French, of about 1550, with monograms of Henry II. This is at South Kensington.

The contrivance of placing a string or two at the side of the finger-board is evidently very old, and was also gradually adopted on other instruments of the violin class of a somewhat later period than that of the *vielle;* for instance, on the *lira di braccio* of the Italians. It was likewise adopted on the lute, to obtain a fuller power in the bass; and hence arose the *theorbo,* the *archlute,* and other varieties of the old lute.

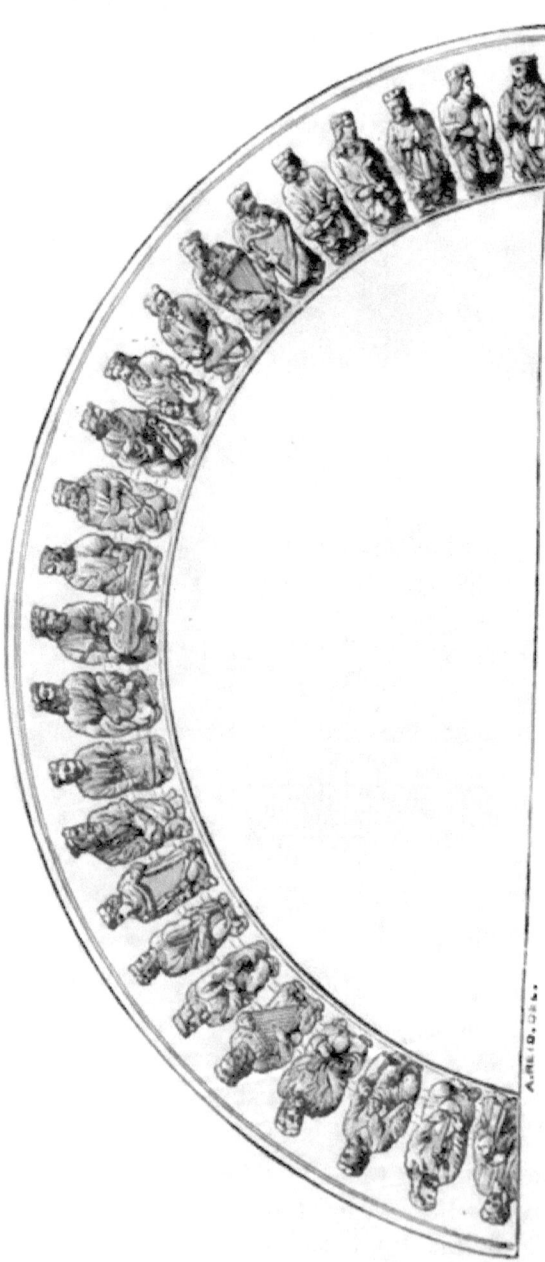

ORCHESTRA, TWELFTH CENTURY, AT SANTIAGO.

A grand assemblage of musical performers is represented on the Portico della gloria of the famous pilgrimage church of Santiago da Compostella, in Spain. This triple portal, which is stated by an inscription on the lintel to have been executed in the year 1188, consists of a large semicircular arch with a smaller arch on either side. The central arch is filled by a tympanum, round which are twenty-four life-sized seated figures, in high relief, representing the twenty-four elders seen by St. John in the Apocalypse, each with an instrument of music. These instruments are carefully represented and are of great interest as showing those in use in Spain at about the twelfth century. A cast of this sculpture is in the Kensington museum.

In examining the group of musicians on this sculpture the reader will probably recognise several instruments in their hands, which are identical with those already described in the preceding pages. The *organistrum*, played by two persons, is placed in the centre of the group, perhaps owing to its being the largest of the instruments rather than that it was distinguished by any superiority in sound or musical effect. Besides the small harp seen in the hands of the eighth and nineteenth musicians (in form nearly identical with the Anglo-saxon harp) we find a small triangular harp, without a front-pillar, held on the lap by the fifth and eighteenth musicians. The *salterio* on the lap of the tenth and seventeenth musicians resembles the dulcimer, but seems to be played with the fingers instead of with hammers. The most interesting instrument in this orchestra is the *vihuela*, or Spanish viol, of the twelfth century. The first, second, third, sixth, seventh, ninth, twentieth, twenty-second, twenty-third, and twenty-fourth musicians are depicted with a *vihuela* which bears a close resemblance to the *rebec*. The instrument is represented with three strings, although in one or two instances five tuning-pegs are indicated. A large species of *vihuela* is given to the eleventh, fourteenth, fifteenth, and sixteenth musicians. This instrument differs from the *rebec* in as far as its body is broader

Front of the Minstrels' Gallery, Exeter Cathedral. XIVth century.

and has incurvations at the sides. Also the sound-holes are different in form and position. The bow does not occur with any of these viols. But, as will be observed, the musicians are not represented in the act of playing; they are tuning and preparing for the performance, and the second of them is adjusting the bridge of his instrument.

The minstrels' gallery of Exeter cathedral dates from the fourteenth century. The front is divided into twelve niches, each of which contains a winged figure or an angel playing on an instrument of music. There is a cast also of this famous sculpture at South Kensington. The instruments are so much dilapidated that some of them cannot be clearly recognized; but, as far as may be ascertained, they appear to be as follows:—1. The *cittern*. 2. The *bagpipe*. 3. The *clarion*, a small trumpet having a shrill sound. 4. The *rebec*. 5. The *psaltery*. 6. The *syrinx*. 7. The *sackbut*. 8. The *regals*. 9. The *gittern*, a small guitar strung with catgut. 10. The *shalm*. 11. The *timbrel;* resembling our present tambourine, with a double row of gingles. 12. *Cymbals*. Most of these instruments have been already noticed in the preceding pages. The *shalm*, or *shawm*, was a pipe with a reed in the mouth-hole. The *wait* was an English wind instrument of the same construction. If it differed in any respect from the *shalm*, the difference consisted probably in the size only. The *wait* obtained its name from being used principally by watchmen, or *waights*, to proclaim the time of night. Such were the poor ancestors of our fine oboe and clarinet.

CHAPTER X.

Post-Mediæval Musical Instruments.

ATTENTION must now be drawn to some instruments which originated during the middle ages, but which attained their highest popularity at a somewhat later period.

Among the best known of these was the *virginal*, of which we give an engraving from a specimen of the time of Elizabeth at South Kensington. Another was the *lute*, which

about three hundred years ago was almost as popular as is at the present day the pianoforte. Originally it had eight thin catgut strings arranged in four pairs, each pair being tuned in unison; so that its open strings produced four tones; but in the course of time more strings were added. Until the sixteenth century twelve was the largest number or, rather, six pairs. Eleven appear for some centuries to have been the most usual number of strings: these produced six tones, since they were arranged in five pairs and a single string. The latter, called the *chanterelle*, was the highest. According to Thomas Mace, the English lute in common use during the seventeenth century had twenty-four strings, arranged in twelve pairs, of which six pairs ran over the finger-board and the other six by the side of it. This lute was therefore, more properly speaking, a theorbo. The neck of the lute, and also of the theorbo, had frets consisting of catgut strings tightly fastened round it at the proper distances required for ensuring a chromatic succession of intervals. The illustration on the next page represents a lute-player of the sixteenth century. The frets are not indicated in the old engraving from which the illustration has been taken. The order of tones adopted for the open strings varied in different centuries and countries: and this was also the case with the notation of lute music. The most common practice was to write the music on six lines, the upper line representing the first string; the second line, the second string, &c., and to mark with letters on the lines the frets at which the fingers ought to be placed—*a* indicating the open string, *b* the first fret, *c* the second fret, and so on.

The lute was made of various sizes according to the purpose for which it was intended in performance. The treble-lute was of the smallest dimensions, and the bass-lute of the largest. The *theorbo*, or double-necked lute which appears to have come into use during the sixteenth century, had in addition to the strings situated over the finger-board a number of others running at the left side of the finger-board which could not be shortened by the fingers, and which produced the bass tones. The largest kinds of theorbo were the *archlute* and the *chitarrone*.

It is unnecessary to enter here into a detailed description of some other instruments which have been popular during the last three centuries, for the museum at Kensington contains specimens of many of them of which an account is given in the large catalogue of that collection. It must suffice to refer the reader to the illustrations there of the cither, virginal, spinet, clavichord, harpsichord, and other antiquated instruments much esteemed by our forefathers.

Students who examine these old relics will probably wish to know something about their quality of tone. "How do they sound? Might they still be made effective in our present state of

the art?" are questions which naturally occur to the musical inquirer having such instruments brought before him. A few words bearing on these questions may therefore not be out of place here.

It is generally and justly admitted that in no other branch of the art of music has greater progress been made since the last century than in the construction of musical instruments. Nevertheless, there are people who think that we have also lost something here which might with advantage be restored. Our various instruments by being more and more perfected are becoming too much alike in quality of sound, or in that character of tone which the French call *timbre*, and the Germans *Klangfarbe*, and which professor Tyndall in his lectures on sound has translated *clang-tint*. Every musical composer knows how much more suitable one *clang-tint* is for the expression of a certain emotion than another. Our old instruments, imperfect though they were in many respects, possessed this variety of *clang-tint* to a high degree. Neither were they on this account less capable of expression than the modern ones. That no improvement has been made during the last two centuries in instruments of the violin class is a well-known fact. As to lutes and cithers the collection at Kensington contains specimens so rich and mellow in tone as to cause musicians to regret that these instruments have entirely fallen into oblivion.

As regards beauty of appearance our earlier instruments were certainly superior to the modern. Indeed, we have now scarcely a musical instrument which can be called beautiful. The old lutes, spinets, viols, dulcimers, &c., are not only elegant in shape but are also often tastefully ornamented with carvings, designs in marquetry, and painting.

The player on the *viola da gamba*, shown in the next engraving, is a reduced copy of an illustration in "The Division Violist," London, 1659. It shows exactly how the frets were regulated, and how the bow was held. The most popular instruments played with a bow, at that time, were the *treble-viol*, the *tenor-viol*, and the *bass-viol*. It was usual for viol players to have "a chest of viols," a case containing four or more viols, of different sizes. Thus, Thomas Mace in his directions for the use of the viol, "Musick's Monument" 1676, remarks, "Your best provision, and most complete,

will be a good chest of viols, six in number, viz., two basses, two tenors, and two trebles, all truly and proportionably suited." The violist, to be properly furnished with his requirements, had therefore to supply himself with a larger stock of instruments than the violinist of the present day.

That there was, in the time of Shakespeare, a musical instrument called *recorder* is undoubtedly known to most readers from the stage direction in Hamlet: *Re enter players with recorders.* But not many are likely to have ever seen a recorder, as it has now become very scarce: we therefore give an illustration of this old instrument, which is copied from "The Genteel Companion; Being exact Directions for the Recorder: etc." London, 1683.

The *bagpipe* appears to have been from time immemorial a special favourite instrument with the Celtic races; but it was perhaps quite as much admired by the Slavonic nations. In Poland, and in the Ukraine, it used to be made of the whole skin of the goat in which the shape of the animal, whenever the bagpipe was expanded with air, appeared fully retained, exhibiting even the head with the horns; hence the bagpipe was called *kosà*, which signifies a goat. The woodcut p. 120 represents a Scotch bagpipe of the last century.

The bagpipe is of high antiquity in Ireland, and is alluded to in Irish poetry and prose said to date from the tenth century. A pig gravely engaged in playing the bagpipe is represented in an illuminated Irish manuscript, of the year 1300 : and we give p. 121

a copy of a woodcut from " The Image of Ireland," a book printed in London in 1581.

The *bell* has always been so much in popular favour in England that some account of it must not be omitted. Paul Hentzner a German, who visited England in the year 1598, records in his journal: " The people are vastly fond of great noises that fill the ear, such as the firing of cannon, drums, and the ringing of bells; so that in London it is common for a number of them that have got a glass in their heads to go up into some belfry, and ring the bells for hours together for the sake of exercise." This may be exaggeration,—not unusual with travellers. It is, however, a fact that bell-ringing has been a favourite amusement with Englishmen for centuries.

The way in which church bells are suspended and fastened, so as to permit of their being made to vibrate in the most effective manner without damaging by their vibration the building in which they are placed, is in some countries very peculiar. The Italian *campanile*, or tower of bells, is not unfrequently separated from the church itself. In Servia the church bells are often hung in a frame-work of timber built near the west end of the church. In Zante and other islands of Greece the belfry is usually separate from the church. The reason assigned by the Greeks for having adopted this plan is that in case of an earthquake the bells are likely to fall and, were they placed in a tower, would destroy the roof of the church and might cause the destruction of the whole building. Also in Russia a special edifice for the bells is generally separate from the church. In the Russian villages the

bells are not unfrequently hung in the branches of an oak-tree near the church. In Iceland the bell is usually placed in the lych-gate leading to the graveyard.

The idea of forming of a number of bells a musical instrument such as the *carillon* is said by some to have suggested itself first to the English and Dutch; but what we have seen in Asiatic countries sufficiently refutes this. Moreover, not only the Romans

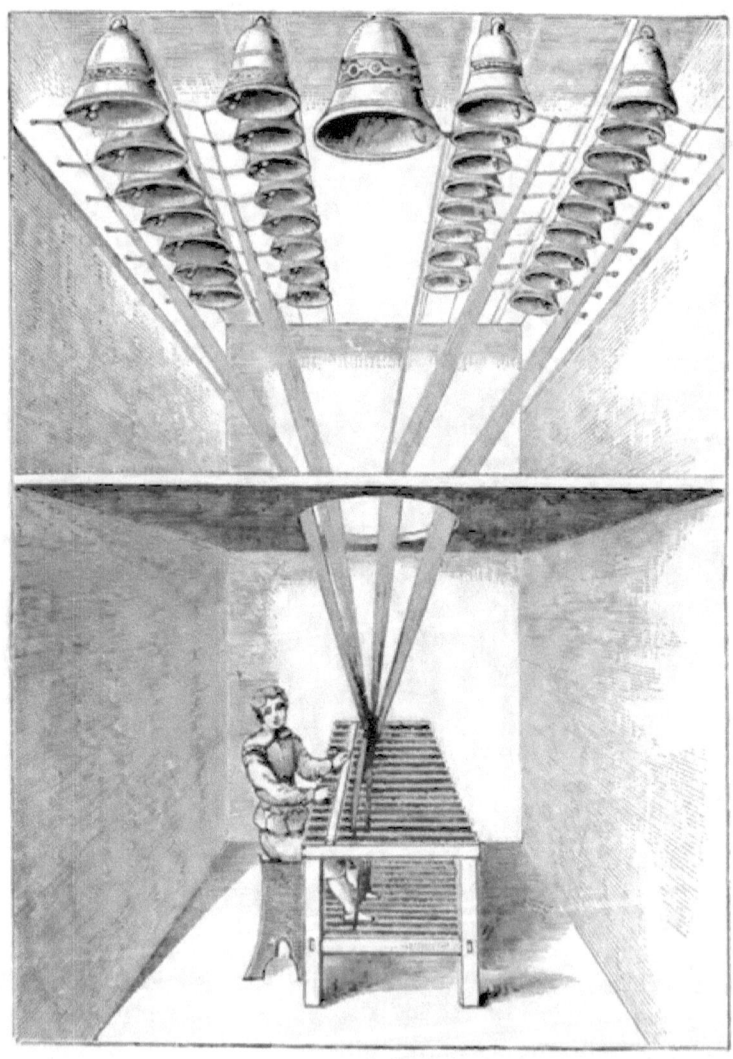

employed variously arranged and attuned bells, but also among the Etruscan antiquities an instrument has been discovered which is constructed of a number of bronze vessels placed in a row on a metal rod. Numerous bells, varying in size and tone, have also been found in Etruscan tombs. Among the later contrivances of this kind in European countries the sets of bells suspended in a wooden frame, which we find in mediæval illuminations, deserve notice. In the British museum is a manuscript of the fourteenth century in which king David is depicted holding in each hand a hammer with which he strikes upon bells of different dimensions, suspended on a wooden stand.

It may be supposed that the device of playing tunes by means of bells merely swung by the hand is also of ancient date. In Lancashire each of the ringers manages two bells, holding one in either hand. Thus, an assemblage of seven ringers insures fourteen different tones; and as each ringer may change his two notes by substituting two other bells if required, even compositions with various modulations, and of a somewhat intricate character, may be executed,—provided the ringers are good timeists; for each has, of course, to take care to fall in with his note, just as a member of the Russian horn band contributes his single note whenever it occurs.

Peal-ringing is another pastime of the kind which may be regarded as pre-eminently national to England. The bells constituting a peal are frequently of the number of eight, attuned to the diatonic scale. Also peals of ten bells, and even of twelve, are occasionally formed. A peculiar feature of peal-ringing is that the bells, which are provided with clappers, are generally swung so forcibly as to raise the mouth completely upwards. The largest peal, and one of the finest, is at Exeter cathedral: another celebrated one is that of St. Margaret's, Leicester, which consists of ten bells. Peal-ringing is of an early date in England; Egelric, abbot of Croyland, is recorded to have cast about the year 960 a set of six bells.

The *carillon* (engraved on the opposite page) is especially popular in the Netherlands and Belgium, but is also found in

Germany, Italy, and some other European countries. It is generally placed in the church tower and also sometimes in other public edifices. The statement repeated by several writers that the first carillon was invented in the year 1481 in the town of Alost is not to be trusted, for the town of Bruges claims to have possessed similar chimes in the year 1300. There are two kinds of carillons in use on the continent, viz.: clock chimes, which are moved by machinery, like a self-acting barrel-organ; and such as are provided with a set of keys, by means of which the tunes are played by a musician. The carillon in the ' Parochial-Kirche' at Berlin, which is one of the finest in Germany, contains thirty-seven bells; and is provided with a key-board for the hands and with a pedal, which together place at the disposal of the performer a compass of rather more than three octaves. The keys of the manual are metal rods somewhat above a foot in length; and are pressed down with the palms of the hand. The keys of the pedal are of wood; the instrument requires not only great dexterity but also a considerable physical power. It is astonishing how rapidly passages can be executed upon it by the player, who is generally the organist of the church in which he acts as *carilloneur*. When engaged in the last-named capacity he usually wears leathern gloves to protect his fingers, as they are otherwise apt to become ill fit for the more delicate treatment of the organ.

The want of a contrivance in the *carillon* for stopping the vibration has the effect of making rapid passages, if heard near, sound as a confused noise; only at some distance are they tolerable. It must be remembered that the *carillon* is intended especially to be heard from a distance. Successions of tones which form a consonant chord, and which have some duration, are evidently the most suitable for this instrument.

Indeed, every musical instrument possesses certain characteristics which render it especially suitable for the production of some particular effects. The invention of a new instrument of music has, therefore, not unfrequently led to the adoption of new effects in compositions. Take the pianoforte, which was invented in the beginning of the eighteenth century, and which has now obtained so great a popularity: its characteristics inspired our great composers to the invention of effects, or expressions, which cannot be properly rendered on any other instrument, however superior in some respects it may be to the pianoforte. Thus also the improvements which have been made during the present century in the construction of our brass instruments, and the invention of several new brass instruments, have evidently been not without influence upon the conceptions displayed in our modern orchestral works.

Imperfect though this essay may be it will probably have convinced the reader that a reference to the history of the music of different nations elucidates many facts illustrative of our own musical instruments, which to the unprepared observer must appear misty and impenetrable. In truth, it is with this study as with any other scientific pursuit. The unassisted eye sees only faint nebulæ where with the aid of the telescope bright stars are revealed.

INDEX.

Al-Farabi, a great performer on the lute, 57
American Indian instruments, 59, 77
   ,,   value of inquiry, 59
   ,,   trumpets, 67
   ,,   theories as to origin from musical instruments, 80
Arab instruments very numerous, 56
Archlute, 109, 115
Ashantee trumpet, 2
Asor explained, 19
Assyrian instruments, 16
"Aulos," 32

Bagpipe, Hebrew, 23
   ,,   Greek, 31
   ,,   Celtic, 119
Barbiton, 31, 34
Bells, Hebrew, 25
   ,,   Peruvian, 75
   ,,   and ringing, 121—123
Blasius, Saint, the manuscript, 86
Bones, traditions about them, 47
   ,,   made into flutes, 64
Bottles, as musical instruments, 71
Bow, see Violin
Bruce, **his discovery of harps on frescoes, 11**

Capistrum, 35
Carillon, 121, 124
Catgut, how made, 1
Chanterelle, 114
Chelys, 30
Chinese instruments, 38
   ,,   bells, 40
   ,,   drum, 44
   ,,   flutes, 45
   ,,   board of music, 80
Chorus, 99

Cimbal, or dulcimer, 5
Cithara, 86
   ,,   Anglican, 92
Cittern, 113
Clarion, 113
Cornu, 36
Crowd, 94
Crwth, 34, 93
Cymbals, Hebrew, 25
   ,,   or cymbalum, 105
   ,,   113

David's (King) private band, 19
   ,,   his favourite instrument, 20
Diaulos, 32
Drum, Hebrew, 24
   ,,   Greek, 32
   ,,   Chinese, 44
   ,,   Mexican, 71, 73
Dulcimer, 5
   ,,   Assyrian, 17
   ,,   Hebrew, 19
   ,,   Persian prototype, 54

Egyptian **(ancient) musical instruments,** 10
Egyptian harps, 11
   ,,   flutes, 12
Etruscan instruments, 33
   ,,   flutes, 33
   ,,   trumpet, 33

Fiddle, originally a poor contrivance, 50
Fiddle, Anglo-saxon, 95
   ,,   early German, 95
Fistula, 36
Flute, Greek, 32
   ,,   Persian, 56
   ,,   Mexican, 63

MUSICAL INSTRUMENTS. 127

Flute, Peruvian, 63
  ,, mediæval, 100
"Free reed," whence imported, 5

Gerbert, abbot, 86
Greek instruments, 27
  ,, music, whence derived, 27

Hallelujah, compared with Peruvian song, 82
Harmonicon, Chinese, 42
Harp, Egyptian, 11
  ,, Assyrian, 16
  ,, Hebrew, 19
  ,, Greek, 28
  ,, Anglo-saxon, 89
  ,, Irish, 90
Hebrew instruments, 19, 26
  ,, pipe, 22
  ,, drum, 24
  ,, cymbals, 25
  ,, words among Indians, 83
Hindu instruments, 46—48
Hurdy-gurdy, 107
Hydraulos, hydraulic organ, 33

Instruments, curious shapes, 2
  ,, value and use of collections, 4, 5, 7
Instruments, Assyrian and Babylonian, 18

Jubal, 26
Juruparis, its sacred character, 68

Kinnor, 20
King, Chinese, 39
  ,, various shapes, 40

Lute, Chinese, 46
  ,, Persian, 54
  ,, Moorish, 57
  ,, Elizabethan, 114
Lyre, Assyrian, 17
  ,, Hebrew, 19
  ,, ,, of the time of Joseph, 21
Lyre, Greek, 29, 30
  ,, Roman, 34
  ,, ,, various kinds, 34
  ,, early Christian, 86
  ,, early German "*lyra*," 95

Magadis, 27, 31
Magrepha, 23
Maori trumpet, 2

Materials, commonly, of instruments, 1
Mediæval musical instruments, 85
  ,, ,, ,, derived from Asia, 85
Mexican instruments, 60
  ,, whistle, 60
  ,, pipe, 61, 81
  ,, flute, 63
  ,, trumpet, 69, 82
  ,, drum, 71
  ,, songs, 79
  ,, council of music, 80
Minnim, 22
Monochord, 98
Moorish instruments adopted in England, 56
Muses on a vase at Munich, 30
Music one of the fine arts, 1

Nablia, 35, 88
Nadr ben el-Hares, 54
Nareda, inventor of Hindu instruments, 46
Nero coin with an organ, 34
Nofre, a guitar, 11

Oboe, Persian, 56
Oliphant, 101
Orchestra, 107
  ,, modifications, 7
Organistrum, 98, 111
Organ, 101
  ,, pneumatic and hydraulic, 101
  ,, in MS. of Eadwine, 103

Pandoura, 31
Pedal, invented, 103
Persian instruments, 51
  ,, harp, 51
Peruvian pipes, 65
  ,, drum, 74
  ,, bells, 75
  ,, stringed instruments, 77
  ,, songs, 78, 79
Peterborough paintings of violins, 95
Pipe, single and double, 22
  ,, Mexican, 61
  ,, Peruvian, 65
Plektron, 30
Poongi, Hindu, 51
Pre-historic instruments, 9
Psalterium, 35, 87, 89, 111, 113

Rattle of Nootka Sound, 2
  ,, American Indian, 74

Rebeck, 94, 113
Recorder, 119
Regal, 103
Roman musical instruments, 34
" lyre, 34
Rotta, or rote, 91, 92

Sackbut, 101, 113
Sambuca, 35
Santir, 5, 54
Sêbi, the, 12
Shalm, 113
Shophar, still used by the Jews, 24
Sistrum, Hebrew, 25
" Roman, 37
Songs, Peruvian and Mexican, 79
Stringed instruments, 3
Syrinx, 23, 113
" Greek, 32
" Roman, 36
" Peruvian, 64, 81

Tamboura, 22, 47
Temples in China, 46
Theorbo, 109, 115
Tibia, 35
Timbrel, 113
Tintinnabulum, 106
Triangle, 106
Trigonon, 27, 30, 35

Trumpet, Assyrian, 18
" Hebrew, 24
" Greek, 32
" Roman, 36
" American Indian, 67
" of the Caroados, 69
" Mexican, 69, 82
Tympanon, 32

Universality of musical instruments, 1

Vielle, 107, 108
Vihuela, 111
Vina, Hindu, 47
" performer, 48
Viol, Spanish, 111, 117
" da gamba, 117
Violin bow invented by Hindus? 49
" Persian, 56
" mediæval, 95
Virginal, 114

Wait, the instrument, 113
Water, supposed origin of musical instruments, 47
Whistle, prehistoric, 9
" Mexican, 60
Wind instruments, 3

Yu, Chinese stone, 39
" " wind instrument, 45

THE END.

DALZIEL AND CO., CAMDEN PRESS, N.W.

www.ingramcontent.com/pod-product-compliance
Lightning Source LLC
Chambersburg PA
CBHW020101170426
43199CB00009B/356